THE GREAT
SHERLOCK
HOLMES
PUZZLE BOOK

THE GREAT SHERLOCK HOLMES PUZZLE BOOK

A collection of enigmas to puzzle even the greatest detective of all

Dr. Gareth Moore

ARCTURUS

ARCTURUS

This edition published in 2020 by Arcturus Publishing Limited
26/27 Bickels Yard, 151–153 Bermondsey Street,
London SE1 3HA

ISBN: 978-1-78828-358-8
AD006093NT

Printed in China

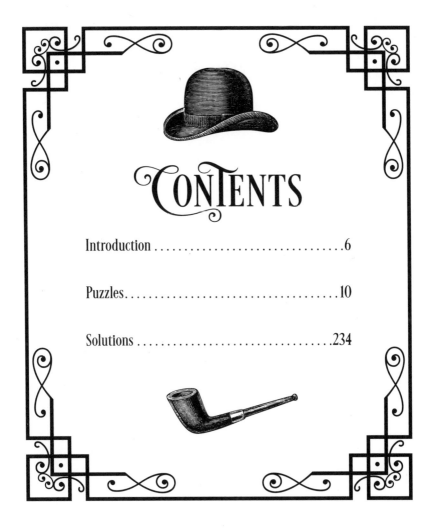

CONTENTS

INTRODUCTION

Dear Reader,

Welcome to this most portentous volume. It is the very first of its kind, for within the pages of this book I have collected together the most unique puzzle vignettes. All have been gathered during the past few years of my life, during which I have had the rare privilege to accompany that most singular of detectives, Sherlock Holmes, on many of his most renowned cases.

Should you somehow fail to have heard of the detective tour de force that is Mr. Sherlock Holmes, let me take a moment to introduce you to him, peccadillos and all.

His signature feature is his towering intellect. His cranial cogitations are majestic in their profundity, often reducing mere mortals such as you, no doubt – and certainly I – to mere observers, no matter how much we might wish to offer some additional insight into his investigatory activities. Having already solved a mystery, he enjoys playing with others in the way that a cat will tease its prey, ensuring that you are never in any doubt as to how superior his own intelligence is to yours. He will frequently challenge you to reach some conclusion or the other, but it is invariably one that he has long ago passed at the wayside in his own insatiable quest for knowledge.

This book collects together more than 130 such challenges that Holmes has set me over recent years, and which I present here in written form for your edification and entertainment.

These challenges are of several different types. Some rely on principles of the mathematical kind, while many need one or more logical deductions to be made from the presented writings. A few make reference to contemporary technology or other new inventions of our Victorian era, and others require abstract thinking to explain some apparently impossible situation. Let me assure you, however, that none require any special knowledge or experience, beyond the wit that God himself gave you as you entered this mortal world.

Holmes is rather fond of riddles, so I should also take this opportunity to give you fair warning that at least a few of the challenges require cleverness of the language variety, with a few plays on words and the like. If a puzzle seems unsolvable, it is always worth considering that some cleverness is at play and all is not as it seems. I have also seen fit to put a small hint into some of the puzzle titles, so if you should ever find yourself stuck it is always worth considering the true meaning of the title. It might perchance be of some small assistance in your hunt for even the most elusive of answers.

Should any of the conundrums herein happen to challenge and perplex you beyond your ken, I have (much against Holmes's recommendation, I might add) included full solutions at the back of this volume. Here I have stated the answer as it was originally given to me. This section might, I suggest, be given to a friend or detective

colleague to read, so that they can concoct a hint that is slightly less fiendish than those already given to you on the puzzle pages.

Each challenge may be tackled on its own, and you may dip in and out of the book at your leisure. The material tells no grand overall story, beyond documenting the genius of the man I am lucky to call my friend: Mr. Sherlock Holmes.

Doctor John Watson,
221B Baker Street, London, 1897

THE FIRST DEDUCTION

Holmes and I met with some of the Baker Street Irregulars to discuss a case. Before we arrived at the meeting place, he remarked that we were meeting with three boys who had worked with us before: Tom, Mickey and Joe. The names rang bells, but I could not immediately remember which was which.

"Which cases did they help us with again, Holmes?" I asked, hoping that this would jog my memory.

"Oh, let me see, Watson. It was – if I remember your case names correctly – The Crimson Consideration, The Mark of Three, and The Case of the Vanishing Glass."

This helped me a little, and I recalled a connection between The Mark of Three and the name Joe. But I still could not picture him, and as for the remaining two boys, I had no idea which cases they had assisted us with.

When we arrived at our meeting, I realized that I did indeed recognize all three boys. One had a mole on his chin, another a scar beneath his eye, and the third had wild, bushy hair that sprang out from his head at all angles. I was confident that the one with the scar was Mickey, as I remembered a story about his brother giving him the scar in a fight. It was then that I remembered his impressive bushy hair had featured heavily in my account of The Case of the Vanishing Glass.

From these somewhat paltry recollections, I am pleased to say I was able to greet each boy by the correct name, and make some polite remark about the case he had helped us with.

Can you deduce which name belonged to which boy, and on which case he worked?

A SPECIAL NUMBER

Holmes once asked me, "Watson, do you have a preferred number?"

I thought about it for a moment, then answered, "I suppose I rather like three. It has something of a pleasing quality to it."

Holmes replied with a shake of his head, before proclaiming, "Where is your sense of adventure, Watson? Such a small number, and so little that can be said about it! Now tell me, what do you make of the number 8,549,176,320? It is a rather special one, if you ask me."

Indeed, it was. But why was it so special?

THE FAST TRAIN

A friend of mine works and lives in the city, but rather enjoys a jaunt to the countryside whenever possible. Each weekend, he heads off to King's Cross station around Saturday lunchtime and catches either the train to Leicester or the train to Dover, taking whichever is leaving first. Both run at perfect twenty minute intervals, but even though the exact time of his arrival at the station is random, he has found that around 90 per cent of the time he ends up in Leicester rather than Dover.

I reported this oddity to Holmes, who was of course immediately able to shed light on it.

What was the explanation?

THE CASE OF
THE RED WIDOW

"Watson," asked Holmes, "did I ever tell you about the case of the Red Widow?"

"No," I answered, "but pray do."

"It was 1879, and I had not long been in the detective business when I heard that the Earl of Buckinghamshire had been plagued by the ghostly vision of a woman. He had seen her, framed in a doorway, wearing a glowing red dress – and then as he watched she melted away, fading ethereally into the whitewashed walls beyond."

"Goodness, Holmes," I exclaimed. "The man must have been mad. Both you and I know with perfect certainty that no inhabitant of the spectral realm has ever been proven to exist."

"I assure you, dear Watson, that the man was perfectly sane. What he had seen, however, was indeed not a ghost but rather a physical manifestation planted firmly within the terra firma of our own humble existence.

"If I were to continue and tell you that I later located the woman in entirely corporeal form, and that when the Earl had seen her she had been wearing a vivid, green dress on a bright, sunny day, can you venture an explanation as to what had truly transpired?"

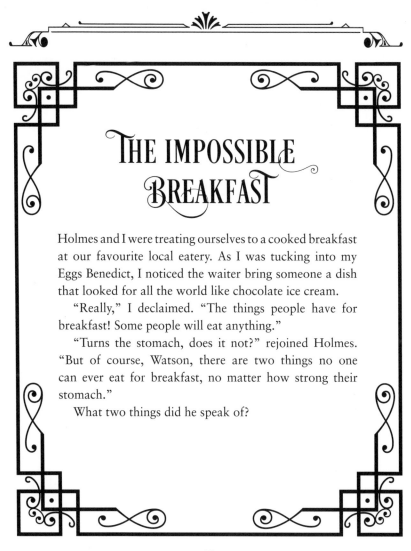

The Impossible Breakfast

Holmes and I were treating ourselves to a cooked breakfast at our favourite local eatery. As I was tucking into my Eggs Benedict, I noticed the waiter bring someone a dish that looked for all the world like chocolate ice cream.

"Really," I declaimed. "The things people have for breakfast! Some people will eat anything."

"Turns the stomach, does it not?" rejoined Holmes. "But of course, Watson, there are two things no one can ever eat for breakfast, no matter how strong their stomach."

What two things did he speak of?

FOUR BY FOUR

"Here's an interesting little mathematical puzzle for you, Watson," said Holmes one day. "Can you find a way to make every whole number from 0 to 20 using exactly four 4s and whichever mathematical operations you wish?"

He gave me the example '$0 = \frac{4}{4} - \frac{4}{4}$' to start me off, but I then must admit it I rather struggled on some of the remaining numbers.

How well can you do, dear reader?

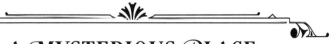

A MYSTERIOUS PLACE

Holmes and I were in Bedfordshire on a case. There had been a break-in at an old estate, and yet the muddy footprints found at the scene did not match any of the soil types in close proximity to the building. As a result, we went for an exploratory walk in the surrounding area, with Holmes bending down to pinch a little earth between his fingers every now and again.

Our journey was notable for its eerie quietude. We passed not a soul as we walked, and when we eventually reached the main road, there was not a vehicle in sight.

"It's like the land of the dead out here," I remarked.

"Watson," Holmes said, "you're a reasonably well-journeyed man, are you not?"

"Well yes, I suppose I am," I replied. "More so than your average London gentleman, I would venture."

"In that case, I am sure this is not the first time that you have come across a place that has roads without vehicles, streets without people, and rivers without a single living creature in them."

I scratched my head. "I can't say that I have, Holmes. Even in the quietest of places, there's always a person or two about, or a few tiddlers swimming in a stream."

But when he told me of the place he had in mind, I realized that of course I was familiar with it, and had in fact spent many a happy hour exploring its reaches. What was it?

THE
PRESENT-PACKING
POSER

One year I had intended to ship some Yuletide presents to relatives of mine who were then living in the south of France. At the Baker Street Post Office, they informed me that the delivery would be charged by the number of shipping crates, but that each crate could carry 25 pounds. Now I happened to have precisely 75 pounds of goods, so naturally I wanted to use only three crates. My parcels were of the following weights: 1 pound, 2 pounds, 2 pounds (again), 4 pounds, 8 pounds, 9 pounds, 10 pounds, 11 pounds, 13 pounds and 15 pounds.

Did I manage to pack all of these parcels into three crates, without exceeding the weight limit of any one crate?

GREAT NIECES AND GREAT NEPHEWS

"My niece Beatrice gave birth again last week," Mrs. Hudson announced one day. "And would you believe it? Another girl!"

Holmes and I exchanged a look. Mrs. Hudson had rather a large number of nephews and nieces, not to mention a rapidly expanding plethora of great nephews and great nieces, and it was

becoming increasingly hard to keep track of who was who, or indeed who was whose.

"Indeed! How many children does Beatrice now have?" I enquired.

"That's her fourth! And Agatha has three, but again all daughters and not a boy in sight. I do declare we need some kind of rule to stop them having any more girls until we've had some boys!"

I pondered this for a moment, before suggesting, "Perhaps there should be a general rule that once a family eventually has a boy, they must stop having children lest they later have a girl. That'll give the boys a chance to catch up."

Here, Holmes interjected. "But that would make not the slightest difference at all, Watson."

He was quite right, of course. Can you explain why?

The Barrel Quarrel

Holmes and I were having a quiet post-case drink at the local pub when we happened to overhear a disagreement between the landlord and a customer. The customer was buying what was left in a particular barrel of beer, and insisted that the barrel was less than half full and he should be charged accordingly. The landlord, meanwhile, maintained that it was more than half full and he wished to charge the customer accordingly. Fortunately for them, Holmes was able to help them resolve the question without using any measuring equipment.

How did he do it?

BROTHERS AND SISTERS

One day I asked our resident
housekeeper, "Your nieces both
have several children, do they not,
Mrs. Hudson?"

"Oh, yes," she replied.
"Beatrice has four
daughters and no
sons, but Agatha has
only three daughters,
although each of Agatha's
daughters has one brother."

"So, Watson," quizzed Holmes,
"which of them has the greater
number of children?"

READING ROOM

As with his thoughts on so many things, Holmes' idea of a holiday is rather strange. The most recent example of this was last summer, when he decided that a rural stay in a basic wooden cabin was the luxury to which he truly aspired.

Upon his return, I asked him how he had enjoyed his sojourn.

"Most excellent," he replied. "The lack of so many of life's modern distractions allowed me to solve several historical cases that had been troubling me. With no running water, and no electric or gas lights, and indeed not even a proper bed, a mattress on the floor was all I needed to read through the case notes that I had brought with me."

"Goodness!" I rejoined. "So a fire was your only source of light? For reading your notes, I mean? Surely you strained your eyes?"

"But not at all. In fact, I had no ready means to light such a fire, even if I had wished to. The nights were quite hot enough without such an encumbrance."

If Holmes had no electricity or gas lighting, and no means of lighting a fire, how was he able to see well enough to read?

The Three Feet Feat

"I happened upon a three-legged donkey earlier today," I informed Holmes one afternoon. "The joke among us passers-by was that it was no longer a 'donkey', but rather now a 'wonky'."

"Very droll," Holmes remarked. "But I can do you one better. I saw something today with three feet and no legs. Can you tell me what it was?"

Indeed – what was it?

A FIRST KEYBOARD
CONUNDRUM

"Watson," said Holmes, "you see that typewriter in the corner of the room? The one you use to write those fantastical reports of my detecting activities?"

"Why yes," I said, "although I say again that my reports do not in any way sensationalize your prodigious talents."

"Have you ever given thought to the longest word you could type with it?"

This seemed to me rather a bizarre question, until Holmes followed up shortly with: "What do you think the longest word you can type on the top row of that mechanical keyboard is? The one that reads QWERTYUIOP?"

And indeed, I pondered – what is the longest word I could type?

The Cuboid Calendar

Early one January morning, I discovered that Holmes had not troubled himself with obtaining a new calendar for the new year. This was most inconvenient for me, as I like to keep a clear track of dates so that all my writings retain the correct chronology, for the best interests of my readers.

When I brought this to Holmes' attention, he went over to the basket of wood by the fireplace and picked out four large wooden cubes.

"Paint on these, Watson," he said, "and you'll be

able to keep track of the date for ever more."

"Whatever do you mean?" I asked him.

He picked up a cube. "On this one you can write the names of the first six months, using one face for each month. On a second cube, you can write the other six. Then use the other two for numbers. Every day you can turn the cubes so that the appropriate date is visible, and that way you can keep track of the days."

This made some vague sense to me, so I set about painting the names of the months on the first two cubes. When I reached the second two, however, I hesitated, convinced that two cubes would not suffice for me to write enough numbers to be able to construct every number from 1 to 31.

Was it possible?

A CAREFULLY CONSTRUCTED NUMBER

"I came across a most pleasing number today, Watson," Holmes once said to me.

"I thought we had established by now that I do not share your capacity to find numbers pleasing," I replied. "They are merely prosaic representations of mathematical certitudes."

"Oh, my dear Watson, I am sure that in this instance you will surely make an exception. For there is a ten-digit number where the first digit is equal to the number of zeros in this magical number; the second digit is equal to the number of ones; the third reveals the number of twos there are; and so on, and so on, right up to the tenth digit, which reveals the number of nines there are."

"I must admit Holmes, that I do not believe such a number could exist. But should it be proven to so do, I would permit that it does indeed sound strangely satisfying."

Holmes was, of course, correct. But what is this mysterious number?

KEEPING UP
WITH THE HUDSONS

"I discovered a rather remarkable thing about Mrs. Hudson's family the other day," Holmes observed.

"Her mother had a sixth finger?" I suggested.

"No, no, I've known about that for years," he replied. "I'm referring to the curious arrangement of her nieces and nephews. Mrs. Hudson's sister has four children, with a three-year age gap between each child and the next. Moreover, the oldest child is currently two-thirds of her mother's age, which is twice what the youngest child's age was last year."

"Well isn't that... something," I replied, somewhat disinterestedly.

"Indeed it is," said Holmes, failing, perhaps deliberately so, to note my lack of enthusiasm. "But tell me, Watson, from this information, can you deduce the age of Mrs. Hudson's sister?"

THE SECRET MESSAGE

While working on a case away from the metropolis of London, Holmes sent me a letter explaining that he believed he was being followed. He required me to send him a certain case file, but he insisted I send it in a locked box, in order to ensure it was not intercepted and read by his putative stalker. Now, it so happened that I had a padlock in the office with which I could lock the box, but I was the only one with the key and so could not get it to Holmes without the same risk of interception. Luckily, Holmes also possessed a padlock, but again he had the key and I did not.

How did Holmes expect me to get the message to him so that he could unlock it, but that no one else could?

THE BAMBOOZLING BACON

One day, Mrs. Hudson was cooking a rather fine breakfast when Holmes overheard her grumbling about the pan being too small.

"Watson," said Holmes, "why don't you help Mrs. Hudson maximize her bacon-frying efficiency?" He then called over to her to ask, "How long does it take to cook a rasher, Mrs. H?"

"I do a minute on each side," replied Mrs. Hudson. "But the pan only fits two rashers at once."

"Ah, but they are perfectly done every time," said Holmes, with one of his rare compliments that he only infrequently offered me. "So, Watson, what is the fastest way for Mrs. Hudson to fry three rashers (this being one rasher for each of us), without cutting any pieces in half?"

THE SECOND DEDUCTION

"This evening I shall be having two of my nieces and two of my great nieces over for tea," Mrs. Hudson told me one afternoon.

"Oh, how lovely, Mrs. Hudson. Which ones?" I asked, despite knowing perfectly well that even if she gave me their names this would in no way help me to recall exactly how they were all related.

"Jane, Margaret, Agatha and Beatrice," she told me, as if with maternal pride.

"What a nice thing to be looking forward to," I said, making a mental note to be well away from Baker Street by the evening. "Do you have any plans for what you intend to do with them? Beyond having tea, I mean?"

"Well, I haven't seen Margaret and her sister in quite a while, so I'm looking forward to hearing all their news. And I've heard that Jane and her aunt had a little disagreement recently, so I'd be interested to hear about it from both sides. Naturally, Agatha will take her daughter's side. And of course Beatrice will tell everyone to listen to me, being the oldest and wisest of the group, but she's only saying that because she's older than the others and wants them to listen to her."

Can you deduce from this information how Jane, Margaret, Agatha and Beatrice are related both to each other and to Mrs. Hudson?

THE PRIMARY SEQUENCE

It was around a year ago, while we were on a case over in Greenwich, that Holmes first began a rather irritating game. Whenever the mood struck him, he would begin a sequence of letters with an undisclosed theme, and would say nothing more to me until I had correctly told him the next letter in the sequence.

As I recall, the first sequence was as follows:

$$M, V, E, M, J, S, \_$$

What did Holmes expect to come next, and why?

A Card Conundrum

During The Case of the Two of Hearts, Holmes and I were on the trail of a serial criminal who had committed a number of crimes in proximity to the establishment that called itself "The Flamin' Aces Casino". We felt sure that the crimes all had a single perpetrator because a calling card was found at the scene of each and every one – a two of hearts.

One evening, after Inspector Lestrade had shown us the stack of cards that the police had collected to date, Holmes turned to me with a question.

"Watson, do you have any interest in probability?"

"Not especially," I answered cautiously. "But why do you ask?"

"Cards always put me in mind of some interesting questions. For example, imagine that you draw two cards from a normal deck of all

fifty-two cards. What is the probability that they are both twos, if I tell you that at least one is definitely a two?"

"Am I to take that example as purely illustrative?"

"Actually, no, Watson. Why don't you have a go at solving it?"

And so, with some reluctance, I did. What was the answer I eventually arrived at?

RED
AND GREEN APPLES

Holmes and I were at the Covent Garden market on an errand to obtain certain fruit and vegetables for Mrs. Hudson.

"Watson," Holmes said. "Here is a question of probability for you."

"Indeed?" I answered, somewhat reluctantly.

"Suppose I give you twenty green apples, twenty red apples, and two large sacks. I instruct you to divide the apples between the two bags in any way you like, using all of the apples. Once you have so done, I will blindfold you, shuffle the sacks, and you will be able to choose one sack and remove one apple. If the apple is red you will win some great reward, whereas if it is green you will bring some great punishment upon yourself. Given these rules, how do you divide the apples so as to maximize the chance that you will pick a red apple?"

Can you determine the best strategy?

EVEN MORE APPLES

Holmes was pleased with his apple-themed puzzle, so he decided to set me another.

"Now, imagine you have a sack of four apples. How can you divide those apples so that you can give one apple each to four people and yet still keep one in the sack?"

THE LONG WALK

"I saw a former associate of mine last week," Holmes told me. "He is an American, but is spending a month's holiday in France."

"He's a lucky man to have such a lengthy holiday!" I replied. "Where in America is he from?"

"Texas," he replied. "And in fact, he told me a rather interesting thing. He happened to mention that he had travelled to Paris from his home in Austin in just over a week, almost entirely on foot. Does that not sound the most remarkable feat, Watson?"

"It sounds remarkably false, I should say. No man is capable of such speed, Holmes."

"You are far too quick to throw around such assertions of impossibility, Watson, as I have told you on many previous occasions. Indeed, I tell you it is not impossible, and I quite believe that he was telling the truth."

How was this feat possible?

SP

ℭLIPPED ẆINGS

Holmes and I were taking a stroll outdoors when a pigeon flew abruptly across our path, causing me to duck.

"Infernal beasts," I said. "Why must our city be so plagued with these flying rats?"

Holmes demurred on my assessment, but then remarked, "This reminds me of an interesting point, Watson," before continuing, "No doubt you are familiar with the phenomenon of flightless birds?"

"Well yes of course," I replied. "The ostrich, the emu and the irrepressible penguin, and not to mention the long-lost dodo. A rather sad state of affairs to have wings which will never fly."

"On that I quite agree," said Holmes. "But can you name an animal which has no wings and yet will one day fly?" He made clear he was not referring to any kind of assisted flight, with hot air balloons or the like.

THE IMPATIENT POCKET WATCH

Holmes and I were walking through the great city of London on our way to a meeting with a prospective client. We had agreed to meet him in the early afternoon at half past one, having set out for our walk at about one o'clock.

"What time is it, Watson?" Holmes asked me.

I pulled out my pocket watch.

"It's…", I began, before following up this grand pronouncement a short moment later with, "Oh!".

"Whatever is the matter, Watson? I will not believe you if you tell me we are running late."

"No – well, actually I am not sure. I had forgotten that my pocket watch has started gaining five minutes for every hour that passes. Look – now it says that the time is six minutes past three."

"And when did you last set it, Watson?"

"It was at five o'clock yesterday evening. I remember hearing the bell ring as I entered 221B Baker Street, and thinking that I must reset it right away."

"Well from that information we can work out the time easily enough."

What time was it?

CELEBRITY CONUNDRUM

"Watson," Holmes said to me one day, "You like to keep in touch with the news, do you not? You are a fickle follower of fame and celebrity, and all that tittle and tattle from the society pages?"

"I suppose I do have a certain interest in the lives of others," I replied cautiously, before adding, "And I might point out that you have occasionally benefitted from my knowledge of society."

"Here's a little puzzle you might enjoy, then," he announced, before continuing with great pomp: "William Gladstone has a long one. Alexander Graham Bell has a short one. Queen Victoria doesn't have one. Casanova always used his. The Pope never uses his."

What was Holmes referring to?

The Third Deduction

I usually keep my notes in case files that live in the drawers of a now rather full filing cabinet, but recently I had cause to keep a couple of them out on my desk in anticipation of writing one of my well-received reports. Unfortunately, Holmes had left the window open and then gone out, and so when I returned home I found the various pieces of paper in a state of disarray, strewn across the floor. This was most frustrating, as the cases had taken place long enough ago that I was unable to entirely remember the details of each one. What I was, however, able to gather from the loose pieces of paper was as follows:

The three cases were to be entitled The Adventure of the Broken Table, The Adventure of the Frozen Lake, and The Adventure of the Moving Statue.

There were three victims, called John Bell, Sarah Doyle and Mark Robinson.

There were three perpetrators, called Juliet Lane, Charlotte Green and Peter Watkins.

The crimes committed were robbery, fraud and murder.

Moreover, between the two of us, Holmes and I were able to remember a few key facts about the cases:

Juliet Lane defrauded her uncle.

Mark Robinson's body was found under a lake that had frozen over.

Peter Watkins was caught because of a splinter in his hand which he'd

obtained from the jagged edge of a dining room table at the crime scene.

Combining these facts together, we were able to deduce the victim, perpetrator and crime committed in each of the three cases. Can you do the same?

THE FIRST REBUS

Holmes and I were investigating a doctor, in relation to a strange series of poisonings that had been going on in North London. The man was absent when we called by his office, so we took the opportunity to look around the premises. We observed that he had made notes next to the names of some of his patients, and one of them read as follows:

I drew this to the attention of Holmes as a subject of possible suspicion.

"I'm afraid I don't think this is going to be much use to us, Watson," was all he offered.

What did the doctor's note say?

LOST AND FOUND

I recently lost my keys to the front door of 221B Baker Street, and spent several hours turning our chambers upside down looking for them. Finally, when they were fully upside down, it occurred to me that perhaps I might have left them in the kitchen when I went to greet Mrs. Hudson upon arriving home the previous day. And, of course, there they were indeed, plain for all to see.

"Why is it," I said to Holmes irritably, "that whenever you lose something, it's always in the very last place you look?"

"Well I should think there's a perfectly good reason for that, Watson."

What reason did Holmes have in mind?

CROSSING THE BRIDGE

I do not recall if I have mentioned before that I am not a particular fan of heights, but it is true. You can perhaps begin to imagine my horror, then, when I discovered that in order to reach a particular client we were required to walk across a rickety old rope bridge across a deep crevasse – and at night, with only one torch between us!

To his credit, Holmes did notice my discomfort and try to take my mind off it, but unfortunately his proposed method of distraction did nothing to make me feel better.

"Consider this, Watson," he said. "The two of us and two others – let us say Mrs. Hudson and Inspector

Lestrade – are attempting to cross a bridge at night, with just a single torch between us. The bridge is a little unstable, so only two of us can be on the bridge at any one time, and none of us is willing to cross without the torch."

"I'm not sure that considering this is going to help me, Holmes."

"Nonsense," he replied. "We have not arrived at the crux of the matter. So, let us say that it takes me one minute to cross in either direction, being physically fit and not particularly fearful. Lestrade takes two minutes to cross in either direction. You, being somewhat more, shall we say, cautious, take five minutes to cross. And dear Mrs. Hudson, being both a little nervous and not in her physical prime, takes ten minutes to cross. What is the shortest time in which the four of us can all cross from one side to the other, bearing in mind that the torch will need to be taken back each time?"

THE SECOND KEYBOARD CONUNDRUM

"Back at the old typewriter again, Watson?" Holmes asked me, as I sat recording our latest case.

"It is my most faithful companion," I responded, before acerbically adding, "and somewhat more reliable than you I might add!"

Holmes ignored the barb, saying, "Yes, yes. Let's resume where we left off, then, shall we? What do you think is the longest word you can type with only the middle row of that keyboard? The one that reads ASDFGHJKL?"

JUGGLING JUICES

Mrs. Hudson was hosting a tea party for her extended family, and she had somewhat optimistically placed Holmes in charge of giving out the food she had prepared while I served the drinks. As I boiled water on the hob to make the many cups of tea that this activity required, and tried desperately to locate enough teacups for the entire party, I observed Holmes perfunctorily tip the biscuits and finger sandwiches Mrs. Hudson had prepared onto a plate that was far too small for them, deposit it dramatically on the table in front of the guests and then swing out of the room with the air of one who has suffered the greatest of indignities.

When I had finally delivered as many cups of tea as there were guests, Mrs. Hudson

announced that in fact since six of the guests were children she would rather they have fruit juice rather than tea. Attempting not to display any irritation due to all of the unnecessary tea I had brewed, I found the bottle of juice that Mrs. Hudson had directed me to, located six glasses and began pouring – but unfortunately I managed to finish the entire bottle after filling just three of the glasses.

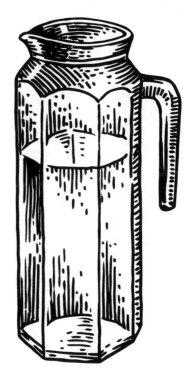

Holmes, who had returned and was now standing around with the air of one who had recently achieved saintliness, came over and found me staring at the row of six glasses, the first three of which were filled and the last three of which stood forlorn and empty.

"Watson," he said, "you have only filled the first three glasses."

"Yes," I replied tersely, "I am well aware of that."

"By touching only one glass, how can you make it so that your row alternates between full and empty glasses?"

How could it be done?

BAGGING BISCUITS

At the tea party I wrote about on the preceding pages, the four youngest children were all very keen to eat as many biscuits as possible, and so to make sure there were some left for everyone else I designated one plate of biscuits specifically for them (having first cleaned up the mess that Holmes had made of serving the edibles).

When the first child came to get his share, he took half of the biscuits on the plate, plus an extra one.

When the second child came to get her share, she took half of the remaining biscuits from the plate, and, again, took an extra one.

When the third child came to get his share, he too took half of the remaining biscuits plus one more.

When the fourth child's turn came, there were no biscuits left, and she promptly burst into tears and had to be given one from another plate.

So how many biscuits were there on the children's plate to begin with?

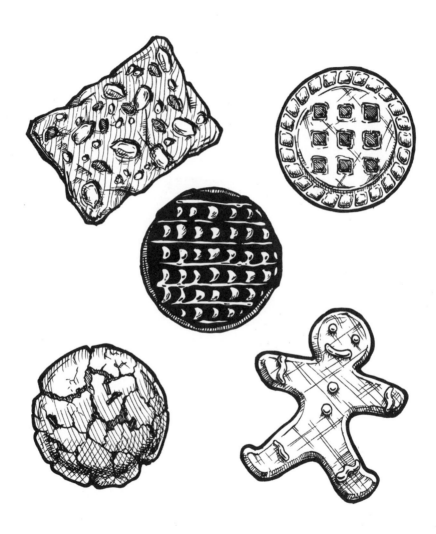

A CODED MESSAGE

One occupational hazard of the detective business is the paranoid client who is certain his every move is being watched. As a corollary of this, Holmes and I have received a rather large number of coded enquiries over the years, which it amuses Holmes to make me decipher.

The first that I shall recount to you read as follows:

CO
MET OFIF
TEE NJUN
IPE RSTRE
ET

What did it say?

ANOTHER CARD CONUNDRUM

I came home to find Holmes absent-mindedly shuffling a deck of cards as he sat in his armchair. The sight of it filled me with a sudden dread, for I knew that some kind of infernal riddle was sure to follow.

"Ah, Watson," he said, without looking up as I came in. "I've been waiting for you."

"I presume you have some kind of pointless card puzzle to torture me with, do you?" I asked.

"Well, that wasn't my intent, but now that you mention it that does seem like rather good sport. So yes. Do you remember our little probability puzzle from last time?"

I sighed. "Yes. You asked me the probability of drawing two twos from a deck of cards, given that one draw was a two."

"Quite right, Watson. Now, here's a fun follow-up. What, would you say, is the probability of drawing two twos from a deck of cards, given that one draw was a two of hearts?"

"Surely the answer is no different from the first case, Holmes? How could it make a difference to know that one card was specifically a two of hearts, rather than just a two?"

"Well, you tell me, Watson."

Does it make a difference? And if so, how?

THE MIXED-UP LABEL

Mrs. Hudson had a rather large number of her extended family over for tea, and during this time a particularly mischievous great nephew took the opportunity to wreak havoc in the kitchen. Seeing that the salt and sugar were kept in identical jars, he managed to find another identical jar in her extensive cupboards and poured alternating layers of salt and sugar into it. The young beast then removed the labels from the existing salt and sugar jars. When his tomfoolery was later discovered, he agreed to reattach the salt and sugar labels, and even

helpfully created a third label that read 'MIXED'. We soon discovered, however, that he had in fact attached each and every label to the wrong jar.

Holmes was very amused by this little prank, and remarked to Mrs. Hudson that in order to rectify the situation she need only taste a single spoonful from one jar.

How could it be done?

The Two Dentists

After an unfortunate incident with a rock cake at a village fête, I found myself in need of an emergency trip to the local dentist while deep in rural England. The small town I was staying in happened to have exactly two such practitioners, and what a remarkable difference between them: one man had a clean and orderly office that it was a pleasure to visit, and greeted me with a broad smile full of dazzling white teeth; while the other lived in a state of total disarray, and though his scowl rarely revealed much of his mouth I was able to discern that it was full of a number of ill-administered fillings.

"So naturally," I later explained to Holmes, "I intend to book an appointment with the former dentist."

"Good heavens, Watson!" Holmes exclaimed. "How could you make such a terrible blunder!"

Why did Holmes think I was making the wrong choice?

THE CIRCULAR PUZZLE

On most weekends Holmes and I find ourselves called away on business, so it is a rare Sunday morning that finds us both sitting and examining that day's papers. When this does happen, however, Holmes often calls out to mock any puzzles he finds among the pages, laughing at what he regards as the childish simplicity of their conundrums.

One morning, though, he summoned my attention away from a particularly fascinating article on a new animal discovered in the far throws of the Empire to show me a new type of puzzle being featured in the paper.

"Look at this circle of letters, Watson," he said. "It is a puzzle so simple that a child can understand it, so I thought you might enjoy it. The aim is to try and create as many words as you can, each of which uses the letter in the middle plus some combination of two or more others. In fact, I've already spotted a rather apt nine-letter one."

What is the longest word you can spot? And how many other words can you find? Holmes professed to have discovered twenty in total.

THE SECONDARY SEQUENCE

Not long after he had set me that first sequence conundrum, I was busy trying to schedule Holmes an appointment at the bank, when with no warning whatsoever he said:

"T, W, T, F, S."

At first I took him to be thinking out loud about a case, but it was only when he refused to elucidate any further that I realized he wanted me to again continue a sequence.

What letter ought I to have said next?

THE FOURTH DEDUCTION

Holmes and I were investigating the theft of a priceless first-edition George Eliot novel from the archives of a local library. The man at the reception desk, however, was extremely old and, as we later discovered, had a rather poor memory of the day of the theft. He could tell us only that three men had visited the archives that day: Brian Pearson, Theodore McNab, and Nicholas Richardson. He knew this only because each visitor had written their names on a different entry form, and so there was no record of the order in which they had visited.

"And you have no recollection yourself of who was your first visitor of that day?" Holmes queried.

"Well, let me see..." The man scratched his chin. "I think the first man had rather a long first name, as when I wished him a good morning he told me to call him by some shortened version of it. I can't tell you

what he looked like, though, I'm afraid – my spectacles were at home and my granddaughter, bless her, didn't bring them in for me until he had left."

"And do you remember anything else at all about that day, or any of these men?"

Holmes showed the man the list of the three names he had made.

"Well, let me see…" said the man, now scratching his head. "Nicholas Richardson. I liked him. He was dressed very smartly, you see, taking things seriously. Much better than this other man we'd had earlier in the day, who was dressed in overalls, would you believe? Hardly appropriate clothes for the archive, if you ask me."

"You thought this man in overalls was suspicious?"

"Oh, yes." The old man looked positively gleeful. "I had an intuition about him, Mr. Holmes. I thought to myself, 'He's not a man to be trusted.' That's why I stayed with him while he was in the archives, sir, to make sure the Eliot book was safe. It's our greatest treasure you know."

"Aha. Well, thank you very much for your help, sir," said Holmes. "I now know who stole the book, and I am sure it will be recovered soon."

Can you deduce, as Holmes did, which of the three men stole the book, and when he visited?

THE SAME TEA

While we were on a case in a distant part of the city, we partook of a late breakfast at a somewhat run-down café, where Holmes was rather annoyed to notice a fly in his tea. He summoned over the waiter and asked to be brought a new cup, at which the waiter took his tea and hurried off in the direction of the kitchens.

"Call me cynical, Watson, but I feel certain that fellow will simply remove the fly and then bring me back the same cup."

Shortly, the waiter returned with a fly-free cup of tea.

"I do apologise for the mishap, sir," he said, handing it to Holmes.

Holmes nodded in thanks, but moments after the waiter had left us he turned to me and shook his head. "I knew it. The very same tea. That waiter is as lazy as the café is unhygienic."

How did Holmes know it was the same cup of tea?

THE NUT CASE

Being a man of many and varied interests, Holmes subscribes to a number of periodicals. At the beginning of each year he reviews his subscriptions and decides whether to continue with them. On one occasion, he decided to do this while I was present, and called me over to show me the different rates and apparent offers that were available.

"Look at the disparity between these two offers, Watson," he said. "*The Fowl Fanatic* and *The Needlepoint Nut* both have offers designed to attract first-time readers, whereby one pays less than full price for the first four years.

"*The Fowl Fanatic* has a subscription of 40p for the first year, which increases by 20p every year after that for the next three years. *The Needlepoint Nut* has a subscription of 20p for the first six months, which increases by 10p every six months for the next four years. Thank goodness I checked the relative costs before I chose between the two."

"No harm, no fowl," I replied.

But which was the cheaper subscription?

A STRANGE GARDEN

"Watson," said Holmes one day, "I just came across a most curious garden. In one flowerbed, all except two of the flowers were roses; all except two were tulips; and all except two were geraniums."

"Can you tell me how many of each flower there were in the bed?" How many indeed?

COMMON PROPERTY

Recently I came across a scrap of paper with some words idly scrawled on it in Holmes' handwriting. The words were as follows:

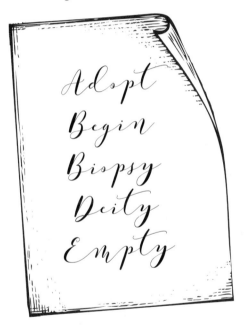

Adopt

Begin

Biopsy

Deity

Empty

What common property do these words share which might have given Holmes cause to write them down?

THE FOUR COINS

Holmes had kindly loaned me some money while we were out one day. I was perturbed to discover upon arriving home that evening that my pockets had been picked and the cash was gone. A few days later, I attempted to return the borrowed amount, but Holmes stopped me.

"Watson, I'm quite happy for you to keep the money."

"That's very kind of you, Holmes, but quite unnecessary, I assure you," I replied.

"I shall make you a deal, then, Watson. I will let you keep the money on one condition." He continued, "Here. You are now holding four pennies in your hand. I will let you keep the original money if you are able to arrange those four pennies so that each one is touching all three of the others."

This task sounded easy enough, so I placed the four pennies flat on the table and pushed them all alongside one another. This was when it became apparent to me that things were more difficult than I had first anticipated, as it seemed impossible to make more than three of them touch at one time. I stared at the coins for quite a while before, finally, inspiration hit.

How did I pass Holmes' test?

HIGH TIME

Holmes and I were passing by the Houses of Parliament at midday, when we heard the familiar chime of the Clock Tower.

"Watson," Holmes said, "have you ever been curious as to the exact height of the Clock Tower?"

"Only mildly, but yes I suppose so," I replied.

Holmes answered with a riddle, as he so often did. "Well, then, it might interest you to know that it is approximately 70 yards plus one third of its total height tall."

How tall is the Clock Tower?

A ONE-WAY ODDITY

One afternoon, while I stayed in to type up some case notes, Holmes had a meeting with Lestrade.

"How did it go?" I asked him, when he returned.

"Oh, you know how it is," said Holmes dismissively. "He tells me his theories about a number of cases he's working on, and I explain to him why they are wrong."

"Of course," I said. "Nothing that might interest my readers, then?"

"Well, I suppose there was something that you might find worthy of note. As we were walking to his office from where we met, we passed a driver going the wrong way up a one-way street. And yet Lestrade did nothing about it."

"Did he not see the man?" I asked. "Or does he simply not consider traffic matters to be his domain?"

"Oh, he certainly saw the man," Holmes replied. "And I'm sure he would have intervened had he believed there had been reason to."

So why didn't Lestrade intervene?

A SIBLING SUM

Mrs. Hudson had her extended family over once again for tea and, as I was in at the time, I decided I ought to try and make conversation.

The first guests I came across were a fairly young boy and girl who I took to be a great nephew and great niece of Mrs. Hudson.

"Are you two brother and sister?" I asked them. They nodded.

"And have you any other siblings?"

"I've got the same number of brothers as sisters," the girl told me.

The boy frowned. "But I've got twice as many sisters as brothers."

How many siblings were there in the family?

The Second Rebus

The Inspector was, as usual, having trouble with a case, and so had sent Holmes a list of suspects to interview, in the hope that he might be able to shed some light on the matter. However, when we arrived at the second house on the list, we found the following message pinned to the door, signed by Lestrade:

What did the message say?

THE DOOR DILEMMA

I recently had the privilege of accompanying Holmes to Buckingham Palace, for an audience with Her Majesty (readers will be disappointed to learn that I am unable to disclose the purpose of our visit). We were met at the palace gates by two guards, one of whom greeted us warmly, shaking our hands in turn, and the other of whom remained sullen and silent, barely acknowledging our arrival. Holmes, evidently amused by this disparity and untroubled by the prospect of insulting the guards by commenting on it, turned to me with an amused expression on his face.

"I say, Watson, this gives me an idea for an excellent riddle."

I tried to wordlessly signal to him that I thought this was neither the time nor the place for riddle-posing, but as ever he was not to be deterred.

"Imagine that there are two doors to a palace: one that leads directly to the throne room and one that takes you straight down to the dungeons. Moreover, these doors are guarded by two guards: one who always tells the truth, and one who always lies. You are in urgent need of an audience with Her Majesty, but when you arrive at one of the doors you do not know whether the guard in front of it is the truth-teller or the liar. What question should you ask the guard to ensure that you are going through the right door?"

THE SHIFTING BOX

Holmes and I were called to Scotland Yard to investigate the appearance of a mysterious box. The box was made of wood, and sealed. It had appeared on the floor of an interrogation room and one of the officers had, with only a small amount of exertion, lifted it onto the table. But since being placed on the table it seemed to have become several times heavier, and now no single officer was capable of lifting it up.

Holmes and I went into the room, where several police officers were guarding the box with suspicion. Holmes walked over to the box and gave the top a sharp knock, making everyone jump. He then tapped the metal table.

"Gentlemen, may I make a guess as to what is inside this box?"

What did he guess?

The Cake Trios

Mrs. Hudson is not perhaps a natural cook, but she has been known to dabble in the baking arts every now and then. On one occasion, she made nine small cakes, storing three each in three tins of different sizes, before later telling us to help ourselves. But before I could tuck in, Holmes interrupted.

"Wait a moment, Watson. Before you devour the cakes, no doubt tin and all, I have a proposition for you. If you can eat three cakes, yet leave each tin still with three cakes in it, then I will give up my share and let you have the remaining cakes."

How could I do it?

WET CLOTHES

I foolishly made the mistake of heading out to the corner shop in mid-November without an umbrella, and naturally on my return it was raining most heavily. I made haste back to 221B but still I became thoroughly drenched. To compound my suffering, Mrs. Hudson was passing through the hallway just as I got back and was not impressed.

"Now, Mr. Watson," she said. "I've just cleaned the carpet and I won't have you dripping all over it."

"What would you have me do instead, Mrs. Hudson?" I asked, wringing my hands as I attempted to wring out my clothes.

"I'll put down some newspaper," she declared. "Just wait there, I won't be a moment."

While all this was going on Holmes overheard our conversation and came down to investigate.

"You're looking rather wet, old chap," he said helpfully.

I sighed. "Yes, I think my clothes were about 99 per cent water after going through that downpour," I told him. "And now, having wrung them out for ten minutes on the doorstep, I think they're now about 98 per cent water."

"There's an interesting question in this," said Holmes. "Let us say that your clothes weighed 20 ounces when you first got here, with 99 per cent of that weight being water. If you've now wrung them out so that only 98 per cent of their weight is water, then how much do they weigh now?"

TAKING THE BISCUIT

I was partaking of a cup of tea with both Holmes and Mrs. Hudson, when Mrs. Hudson produced a plate of biscuits: some plain, some containing raisins, and some containing chocolate chips. She passed them first to Holmes and he selected one containing raisins. Now, quite frankly I have never understood why raisin biscuits need to exist, and I believe that Holmes pretends to enjoy them purely because he knows the disdain I hold them in.

In any case, having made his own dubious choice, Holmes turned to me, saying, "Watson, a challenge! I am considering handing you a biscuit of my own choice. Now, if you can make a true statement about what I am about to do then I will give you that biscuit, but make a false one and I will give you nothing. Now, what true statement can you make to me that will guarantee yourself the biscuit of your choice?"

Given my preference for a chocolate chip biscuit, what statement should I have made?

THE SLOW WORKMEN

Scotland Yard was being refurbished, and a large part of this seemed to involve painting. There were four different men working there, and they seemed to be present at every corner of the building, ready with precarious ladders and large buckets of paint just waiting to be crashed into and tipped over. Moreover, they appeared to be working at an unimaginably slow rate.

"Honestly," I said to Holmes, "I'm certain it's taken them four days to paint just the four walls of the reception room. I dread to think how long it will take for them to finish the building."

I saw from the look on his face that my frustrated comment would not be met in kind, but had engendered in his mind the kind of riddle that I frequently strove to avoid.

"Here's a question for you, then, Watson," Holmes responded. "If it takes four men four days to paint four walls, how many men would it take to paint one hundred walls in one hundred days?"

A SECOND CODED MESSAGE

The second coded message Holmes and I received was a tip-off about an art heist we were investigating. We had so far managed to track down three of four stolen paintings, but the fourth as yet eluded us. That was, at least, until the following message was slipped under our door one day on a torn-off scrap of paper:

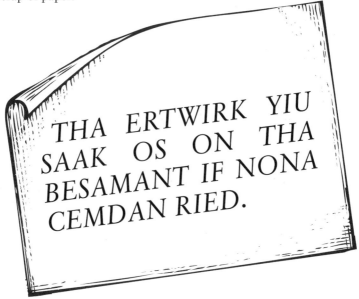

THA ERTWIRK YIU SAAK OS ON THA BESAMANT IF NONA CEMDAN RIED.

So where was the painting?

THE FIFTH DEDUCTION

Scotland Yard had a rather intriguing case for which Holmes and I were called in to consult. There had been a jewel heist and the police were now trying to intercept the jewels as they made their way from the crooks' storehouses to the river docks, before they were smuggled out of the country.

The police had identified four storehouses, one in the North of London, one in the East, one in the West, and one in the South. Moreover, they knew that the four storehouses were shipping their jewels on consecutive days, from Monday through to Thursday. In each storehouse was stashed a different kind of jewel: sapphires in one, emeralds in another, diamonds in the third and rubies in the fourth. In addition, the four crooks involved in the heist, each of whom was taking care of one of the shipments, each had a different codename: Red, Green, Blue or Yellow.

In order to have the best chance of recovering all of the stolen jewels, the police wanted our help in identifying which storehouse contained which type of jewel, when it was planned to ship them, and who was in charge of the shipment.

The officers had managed to retrieve the following set of clues:

The North storehouse will be shipping its product after the rubies have been shipped.

No crook's jewels are the same hue as their codename.

Green's shipment is the final one.

The West storehouse is shipping sapphires one day after Blue's shipment. Yellow's shipment is on Tuesday.

The diamonds are being shipped from the East storehouse, before the emeralds and sapphires.

From this information, can you deduce all of the information that the police require?

AN ODD ORDER

Holmes arrived home at our chambers late one evening, while I was busy reading a most fascinating report in the evening edition of the newspaper that I will perhaps tell you about some other time.

"Watson, there are two men standing outside our front door. A Scot and an Irishman, if I'm not mistaken."

I looked up from my paper with alarm. "Do you think they mean us harm?"

"No, no, I don't think they're here for us at all," he said, to my great relief and minor confusion. "I mention them because of the unusual way they are standing. You see, the Scot was standing behind the Irishman, and the Irishman was standing behind the Scot."

How was this curious arrangement possible?

SLEEPING IT OFF

"My friend told me the strangest story the other day," said Mrs. Hudson, as we joined her for tea. "A cousin of hers was married to a man who was plagued with nightmares about being beheaded. One night, the man was having this same dream again, and just as the axe was being swung his wife tapped him on the back of the neck to wake him up and stop him snoring. Well, the shock of it gave the poor man a heart attack, and he died on the spot!"

"I'm afraid your friend was pulling your leg," said Holmes solemnly.

"Yes," I agreed. "It does sound a bit unlikely."

"Unlikely? I should say it was impossible for it to have happened as Mrs. Hudson reported it."

Why did Holmes think the story could not be true?

THE CASE OF THE SECRET SAILORS

During one of our more fantastical cases, Holmes and I found ourselves investigating the goings-on of a secret society of sailors. After much careful inquiry and coordination with the Baker Street Irregulars, we managed to locate their headquarters. Once inside, we were met with a front desk. Above the desk were two crossed flags and, more curiously, above them was a row of seven clocks. My first thought was that these clocks might be recording the time in different parts of the world, but a quick glance at them made it

clear that this was not the case. From left to right, the clock times were as follows: five past three, half past one, twenty to two, ten to seven, five to ten, twenty to four and five past six.

At the desk was a tall, pallid man in a navy suit. He appeared to appraise us for a moment before saying: "Entry word, please."

Nonplussed, I looked at Holmes, who was of course able to respond immediately.

What was the appropriate password that he was requesting?

GETTING THE CHOP

Holmes and I were investigating a rather shady character who worked as a butcher. Holmes had popped into the shop for some reconnaissance and reported back to me when he returned to Baker Street.

"He's a tall man, Watson – over six feet, at a guess. Strong arms, and mean little eyes."

I noted these details down. "And what does he weigh, would you say, Holmes?"

At this, Holmes smiled. "Why, Watson, I should think that was obvious."

What did the man weigh?

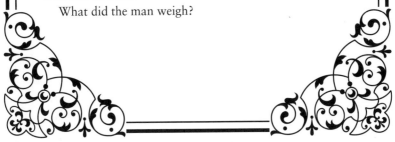

IRREGULAR TWINS

Having spent a fair amount of time with the Baker Street Irregulars, I remarked to Holmes that an unusual number of them were twins.

"Ah yes, well that can come in handy," he replied, "what with the possibility of trading places and so forth."

"Oh dear!" exclaimed Mrs. Hudson, who was sitting with us. "You've reminded me, Mr. Holmes. It was my great niece Jane's birthday yesterday, and I clean forgot all about it!" She stood up abruptly. "It's her twin Margaret's birthday tomorrow. I'd better try and get them both something in time for that."

"Holmes," I said, as Mrs. Hudson hurried off. "Do you think our dear landlady is quite alright? She seems to think that twins can have birthdays two days apart!"

"I have every confidence that Mrs. Hudson is perfectly sound of mind," Holmes reassured me.

But how could it be that one twin's birthday is two days after the other?

SF

A PUDDLE PUZZLE

Standing too close to the carriageway on my way home, I got badly splashed by a passing hackney. Arriving through the door, sopping wet and desperate for a change of clothes, I was met by Holmes. He was typically unsympathetic to my plight, and instead took the opportunity to spring a riddle on me.

"You've reminded me of one of the first riddles I ever heard, Watson. Pray, tell me: what is it that gets wetter as it dries?"

THE STRANGE SHIPWRECK

"Watson," Holmes said, putting down his newspaper one morning, "have you read about the terrible nautical incident that happened yesterday?"

"I'm not sure I have," I replied. "What was it?"

"A boat travelling from America to England sank just off the coast of New York."

"Oh, that is terrible news!" I replied. "How many people were on board?"

"About a thousand people," he said. "But here's a puzzle: where will they bury the survivors?"

I considered this for a moment. "Their place of birth would be the most logical place, I suppose."

"Are you quite sure about that?" Holmes asked, with an arched eyebrow.

What would you suggest?

The Tertiary Sequence

I had hoped, after the first two sequences Holmes sprang on me, that he would give up on the game, but clearly this was his current mental torment of choice. My wishes remaining unfulfilled, he hit me with a third sequence only a month later:

"Y, Y, H, L, Y, E, Y, T, R, R, R."

What comes next in this sequence?

A PALINDROMIC PUZZLE

Curious as to my writing output, one slow weekend I decided to count how many words I had written in a report of a previous case. After many hours counting, during which I rewarded myself with many generous breaks, I finally reached the grand total of 24,942 words. I jubilantly reported this number to Holmes.

"That's a nice palindromic number you have there, Watson," remarked that prodigious brain. "But now that you have at last finished counting, here's something further to consider: how many more words would you have to write in order to reach the next palindromic number?"

Holmes and I were at the dog track, as research for a case that I will certainly report on in full at the soonest opportunity. While we were there, Holmes – in his usual way – could not resist posing me a teaser or two from the expansive, seemingly inexhaustible collection that sits within his brain.

Holmes posed me the following question:

"See how there are eight dogs on the track. Now tell me, Watson, as quick as you can, if a dog begins to outrun the others and overtakes the dog in second place, what place is that dog in now?"

I answered him that of course the dog was now in first place, that being one better than second, to which Holmes responded with nothing more than an arched eyebrow and the following additional teaser:

"If a dog has just overtaken the dog in last position, what position is that dog in now?"

This seemed so obvious that I barely needed to tell him that the dog was now clearly one from last, or in Holmes' specific example with eight dogs it must now be in seventh position.

"Ah, Watson. You have made two false conclusions."

And so I had. What were they?

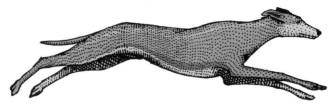

CARNIVAL CAKES

Holmes and I once found ourselves, during one of our investigations, at a village fair. It had a number of amusing games and activities for visitors to participate in, one of which was that most bizarre of sports: guessing the weight of a cake. There was a young couple in front of us, of which the gentleman put in a guess of 57 ounces, while the young lady followed up with a guess of 61 ounces. Holmes went next, and suggested that the cake weighed the more generous sum of 76 ounces. But I, feeling he was likely to be close but may have overestimated a little, put in a guess of 74 ounces.

The fellow running the stall later informed us of the correct weight of the cake, and it transpired that one of us had been 2 ounces out, one of us 4 ounces out, one of us 11 out and the other 15 out. Given this, whose guess had been the closest?

HOLMES, SCRAMBLED

Tired of the constant challenges Holmes was setting me, I decided to set him one of my own.

"Here's a conundrum for you, Holmes. How long a word you can make from your own full name? That is, to say, from the letters SHERLOCKHOLMES?"

"Well, Watson," Holmes replied, "that quite depends. Am I allowed to re-use letters more than the number of times they appear in my name or not?"

I thought about this for a moment. "Well, how about you give me both answers. Both with re-using letters, and without."

After some thought, he responded: "Alright, then. I should say the longest word allowing re-use of the letters is some twelve letters long, although there are a good many more with eleven, and the longest word without re-using letters is nine letters long."

He was, as far as I could ascertain, quite right of course. Can you identify the words Holmes had in mind? Or find words that are almost as long?

MATCHING SOCKS

Early one winter morning Holmes and I were summoned out of the city for an urgent case. Holmes tasked me with packing us both three nights' worth of clothes for the trip, but, out of a desire not to alert the rest of the street to our departure, he refused to turn on the light to enable me to see what I was doing.

Sleep-fuddled and irritated, I called to him angrily from my bedroom.

"You may not care about how you look, Holmes, but I want to give the impression of respectability. That is clearly impossible to do when I can't even see the clothes I'm packing. I've got both white and yellow socks in this drawer, with ten pairs of each. I'm going to have to pack darn near the whole lot to ensure I've got enough matching pairs."

"Nonsense," came the cheery reply from the next room. "Just apply a little mental acuity, my dear Watson, and you'll soon discover you need do nothing of the sort."

How many socks did I need to take from the drawer to ensure that I had three matching pairs?

I found another of Holmes' written collections of words while clearing out a cupboard one day. This time, the words were as follows:

Advocate
Attribute
Contract
Entrance
Project
Refuse

I wondered why he had kept this list, but then I eventually spotted the connection. Can you identify their common property?

AN ILLUMINATING PROBLEM

Holmes and I were investigating a suspected haunting – which turned out, of course, to be nothing of the sort – in a run-down mansion on the edge of the city. There were four switches in the reception room, one of which was for that room's light, but the other three were for rooms which were not visible from the reception room itself. While Holmes was examining the reception room, he tasked me with figuring out which of the switches was for the cellar, where the supposed apparition had been sighted.

"Surely it would be more efficient for you to help me?" I complained, not keen to make the steep descent into the cellar any more times than was necessary.

"Nonsense!" Holmes said. "If you put your mind to it you'll soon see that you need only make one trip."

What method did Holmes have in mind?

A STRANGELY SHAPED RIDDLE

Sometimes Holmes will spring a riddle on me before I even have both my feet through the door:

"Watson," he said, the moment he saw my face, "can you think of an item which comes in a variety of sizes, materials, and shapes, and is straight in some parts and rounded in others? It can be put wherever you may care to put it, and is often lost or misplaced, but there is only one place it truly belongs."

What item did Holmes have in mind?

TRUTH-TELLERS AND LIARS

Holmes values nothing more than the power of pure deductive reasoning, so he is a dedicated enthusiast of that particular breed of logic puzzle involving those who always tell the truth and those who always lie. One I particularly enjoy involves a man visiting an island populated by only such people – let us call them 'Truth-tellers' and 'Liars' – who sees a beautiful woman there who he asks to take to dinner.

The woman replies, "I will go to dinner with you if and only if I am a Truth-teller."

So should the man make a reservation?

THE POISONED PARTY

We investigated a rather unpleasant affair last summer, which involved a number of deaths at a retired colonel's seventieth birthday party. The cause of death was determined to be poison, and Holmes and I did our best to find out from the surviving partygoers whether there was anything that had been consumed in common by all the victims, and no one else, so we could ascertain how the poison had been administered. But out of all the food, there was no item that had not been consumed by both victim and survivor alike, and as for drinks, we established that not all of the victims had drunk the champagne. That left the iced punch, which had, it seemed, been drunk by all the victims, but the Colonel himself had also drunk some and survived.

"And just how much of the punch did you drink?" Holmes asked him.

"Oh, I had a reasonably big glass at the beginning," the Colonel replied. "But after that I didn't have much time for eating or drinking, as I was busy entertaining my guests."

Holmes nodded. "Just as I thought." He turned to me. "Well, Watson, I think we've found the source of the poison."

What was it?

A THIRD CODED MESSAGE

The third coded message Holmes and I received pointed us towards a potential source of information about a murderer, which indeed later turned out to be instrumental.

We had narrowed down our list of suspects to just a few men, when the following message arrived:

?: HE KNOWS
WHO DID IT.

What was the intention of this message?

SUMMATION SORCERY

Holmes and I once caught a con man posing as a magician, who at least had quite a knack for making people's money disappear.

"I have always been fascinated by the work of magicians," Holmes confessed, once we'd handed over our suspect to Inspector Lestrade. "What they do when they construct their tricks is much like a reverse-engineering of the work we do, Watson. While we show how the apparently impossible is possible, they make the possible seem impossible."

"Perhaps you should turn your hand to magic," I suggested. "Detective by day, magician by night. I can picture you quite clearly with a black cape and a magic wand, pulling a rabbit out of a hat."

"I certainly see the attraction," Holmes said, apparently unaware of my teasing. "In fact, I have collected a mental inventory of tricks over the years. But nothing too elaborate," he added. He reached into his coat pocket, rummaged around, and pulled out three dice. "Here's one, for example. Without me looking, I want you to roll these three dice and add up the total, but don't tell me the result."

I rolled them, getting a three, a two and a five, for a total of ten.

"Once you have done that, pick one of the three and find the number on the bottom of the dice, and add that to your total."

I picked up the two, revealing a five at the bottom, and added that, giving me a total of fifteen.

"Now, re-roll that same die, and add the new number to your total."

I re-rolled and this time I got a one, for a total of sixteen.

"Now," Holmes said, turning around. "Remember that I do not know

which of these dice you re-rolled, nor what number it showed to begin with." He looked briefly at the three numbers now shown by the dice. "Your total, if I am not mistaken, is sixteen."

How did he know?

THE ISLAND IN THE LAKE

A mysterious disappearance once took Holmes to a house situated on a tiny island in the middle of a lake in the far north of England. When he got back, he told me of a curiosity he had encountered that he thought I might enjoy.

"On this island, Watson, there was a tractor. The strange thing was, there was not, and never had been, a bridge connecting the island to the mainland, and some enquiries revealed to me that the tractor wasn't taken over by boat or air either, and neither was it assembled on the island. So it was quite the puzzle to me to establish how the tractor had arrived at its current location. Eventually, of course, I did hit upon the answer."

How did the tractor get onto the island?

A FOURTH CODED MESSAGE

The fourth coded message we received came during one of our grizzliest cases: the brutal murder of Christopher Burns. At the time, we had only one suspect: Roger Cardwell, who was a student of Burns and thought to be a little disturbed. After a meeting between the two of them, Burns' body was found in a crumpled heap on the floor, limbs broken, neck bruised and eyes bloodshot.

Despite Holmes' intuitions to the contrary, the police were ready to take Cardwell in, until we received the following message:

RREGOS BEHTORR
SELGNARTD POSSEFORR
BNRUS

Upon decoding this, our investigation was given a new lease of life, and we were eventually able to catch the true culprit.

What did the message say?

USE YOUR HEAD

I came home from a weekend's stay with a friend in the countryside most disgruntled at the discovery that her fourteen-year-old son was now taller than I am.

"A full head taller than me!" I declaimed to Holmes. "It's an embarrassment! I shall have to start wearing shoes with thicker soles to compensate."

Holmes replied, "Well, Watson, I think you're wrong to put stock in such things. But here, let us take your mind off it a little. You have put me in a mind of a riddle."

He then asked me, "What is taller without a head than it is when it has a head on?"

What is the answer?

THE LESSER OF THREE EVILS

"You are a criminal who has been tried and convicted," said Holmes.

"I don't remember that happening," I replied.

"When it comes to the sentencing," Holmes continued, "you are given a choice between three punishments. First, you may be hanged. Second, you may face the firing squad. Or third, you may be locked in a room with lions who haven't been fed for five weeks. Which do you choose?"

Which option would give me the highest chance of survival?

I have always considered myself to be better with children than my famous colleague, but occasionally his powers of deduction can offer entertainment which goes down very well with a younger audience. One of the tricks I most enjoyed myself involved a set of dominoes which some children were amusing themselves with at the house of a client.

"Are you any good at dominoes, Mr. Holmes, sir?" asked one of the children as we passed through the drawing room.

"I have never had much use for the game itself," he replied, "but I do know a couple of tricks associated with it."

Naturally, the children pressed him to show them.

"Alright," he said at last. "Your task is to join the dominoes – like number to like number – so that they form one long line. I will then be able to tell you, without looking at your line, the numbers at either end of it."

He turned his back, and the children got to work joining the pieces.

"We're ready, Mr. Holmes," they proclaimed, mere moments later.

"Your numbers," Holmes declared, "are four and six."

The children erupted in squeals of amazement. But how did he know?

A LIKELY STORY

Mrs. Hudson's mischievous great nephew was once again in Baker Street, but on this visit he graduated to larceny, misappropriating a rather important note from Mrs. Hudson's purse. When we questioned him about it, he professed innocence, saying: "I didn't steal it, sirs. No, I found it in that book over there. She must have used it as a bookmark, and I remember for certain that I found it between pages 47 and 48, poking out the top of the book."

Holmes immediately knew he was lying. How?

THE PARTY PROBLEM

Holmes and I, much to his dissatisfaction, had been compelled to attend a party for the deputy inspector's retirement. Holmes, therefore, felt the need to amuse himself by imposing problems on the assembled dignitaries. One that I particularly enjoyed concerned a large cake that sat portentously on a dais, waiting to be eaten at the conclusion of the evening's festivities.

"Watson, observe that cake. You will note that it is a perfect cylinder of consistent radius from bottom to top, and note also how completely smooth its top surface is. The baker is certainly an artisan. But it also reminds me of a rather satisfying puzzle, that I am sure you will have no trouble demolishing, as you will no doubt later also help demolish the cake itself."

I ignored Holmes' rather unkind reference to my liking for bakery products, and shortly afterwards he continued thus:

"Notice how there are eight people attending this event. Now, say that all eight of those people wish to have an exactly equal amount of cake, how would you best go about this?"

This seemed a not particularly complex challenge, until he also added:

"You may only use three cuts, and all eight pieces must be of the same shape and size."

What solution did he have in mind?

BRIDGE, INTERRUPTED

Holmes and I were invited to a game of bridge at a client's house. Part of the way through a round, the dealer was briefly summoned to another room, and when he returned none of us could remember how far around the table he had got with his dealing. For those uninitiated in the ways of bridge, the dealer must deal 13 cards each to four players, dealing clockwise from a pack of 52 cards.

Can you work out what Holmes' suggestion was for how to rectify the situation? Of course, social decorum had to be maintained and no dealt cards could be touched before the deal was complete, so we could not count how many had already been placed on the table.

ATOP THE SHIPPING CONTAINER

On one particular case, Holmes was determined to examine the top of a large shipping container. The container was far too high for either of us to reach the top on our own, so Holmes suggested that he stand on my shoulders and try to grab the edge of the container and lift himself up.

Not fancying the idea of having Holmes on my shoulders, I objected. "Surely I should stand on your shoulders, Holmes? Lifting oneself up like that is no mean feat, and I think that sort of thing is more my area of expertise, if you don't mind my saying so."

"The physical challenge, of which I assure you I am quite capable, is not the issue, Watson. Even with one of us on the other's shoulders I'm not sure we'll reach the top, but as I am the taller of the two of us we have a better chance if I am on your shoulders."

Why was Holmes correct?

NEWSPAPER PAGES

"Watson," Holmes said to me over breakfast one morning, "how many pages does that newspaper of yours contain?"

I turned to the final page. "36," I told him.

"Nine sheets folded in half then, I imagine. So tell me Watson, if the first sheet of that newspaper contains pages 1, 2, 35 and 36, which pages share a sheet with page 28?"

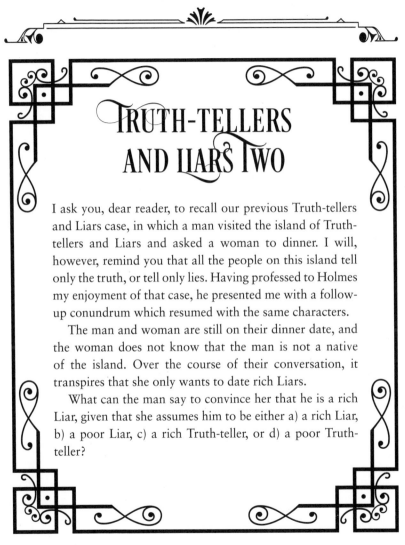

TRUTH-TELLERS AND LIARS TWO

I ask you, dear reader, to recall our previous Truth-tellers and Liars case, in which a man visited the island of Truth-tellers and Liars and asked a woman to dinner. I will, however, remind you that all the people on this island tell only the truth, or tell only lies. Having professed to Holmes my enjoyment of that case, he presented me with a follow-up conundrum which resumed with the same characters.

The man and woman are still on their dinner date, and the woman does not know that the man is not a native of the island. Over the course of their conversation, it transpires that she only wants to date rich Liars.

What can the man say to convince her that he is a rich Liar, given that she assumes him to be either a) a rich Liar, b) a poor Liar, c) a rich Truth-teller, or d) a poor Truth-teller?

Holmes and I were walking through Regent's Park when we saw two young boys limbering up for a race. Amused, we sat on a nearby bench to watch the spectacle. On a count of three they were off, and in not more than about ten seconds of wild running the taller of the two had reached his destination.

"Not exactly neck and neck, was it, Holmes?" I remarked. "I'd say that chap won by a good five yards. Perhaps they'd better apply some sort of handicap next time."

Holmes looked thoughtful. "I'd say they were running about 50 yards in total. So let's say we agree with your estimate that the taller boy won by five yards and, as such, we get him to start the race five yards behind the other. Do you think this measure would even things out?"

I pondered this scenario for a moment. Who would win, assuming they both ran at the same speeds again?

A BANANA BARGAIN

"My gosh! There are some remarkable deals at the fruit market today!" Mrs. Hudson remarked to us on an otherwise unremarkable Tuesday morning. "There's 10 apples and 5 bananas for only 35 pence, saving a total of 5 pence; and there's 30 apples for only 50 pence, saving 10 pence; oh, and, best of all, I found 10 bananas and 10 oranges for only 100 pence. That last deal alone saves you an entire 20 pence."

"Well, Watson," said Holmes, as Mrs. Hudson took the fruits of her fruit-buying into the kitchen. "Based on the information Mrs. Hudson has just given us, could you tell me how much it would ordinarily cost to buy one apple, one banana and one orange?"

TARGET PRACTICE

As has been known to happen on occasion, I came home to find Holmes engaged in revolver practice. A volley of shots went off as I approached the door, so I made certain to knock very loudly before entering.

"Yes, come in Watson!" Holmes called, and then immediately resumed shooting at a target he'd set up on the wall. "I'm getting some shooting practice in."

"Yes, I can see that."

"I'm trying to get my shots down to one every ten seconds," he explained. "But this past minute I only managed six."

"Well then you've done it, haven't you?" I asked.

"I have not, Watson, although I have made some significant progress."

How could Holmes be correct that he'd shot six bullets in sixty seconds and yet had not managed one bullet every ten seconds?

THE BROKEN FIVE

While investigating a case involving a mysterious theft, Holmes and I found ourselves in a printer's typesetting room. There appeared to have been some kind of a struggle, given the state of the furniture in the room, and as I looked around I noticed that thousands of numbers lay strewn across the floor. Most prominent of all was a large number '5', languishing in the middle of the floor.

"Looks like they'll have trouble typesetting any page numbers in the immediate future!" I remarked.

"Perhaps so," agreed Holmes. "In fact, Watson, that raises an interesting question. If you were to write every number from 1 to, let's say, 300, how many times would you write the digit 5?"

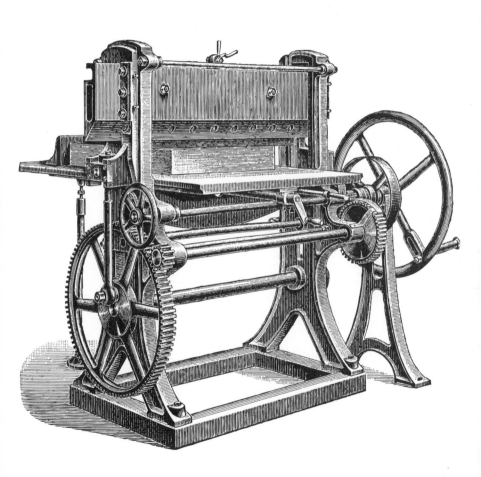

THE TRICKY TESTIMONY

Scotland Yard were investigating a mugging that had taken place in Regent's Park. The victim – a Mr. White – had reported being attacked by a man wearing blue dungarees with paint on the front and a brown cap pulled low over his eyes. The attacker had taken some very valuable items from Mr. White, so a full-scale investigation was launched. A number of people who were known or seen to have been in the park were questioned. One witness reported seeing a man who matched this exact description – cap, dungarees, paint stain – running out of the park towards Baker Street. Unfortunately, as the witness was behind the man, he obtained not even a glimpse of the man's face.

When Holmes heard about this report he frowned.

"I presume you held this witness for further questioning?"

"No, we let him go," said Inspector Lestrade. "He had nothing further to tell us."

"Nothing further?" Holmes exclaimed. "I should say your witness had a lot more to say, considering he lied in his testimony and was quite possibly involved in the crime!"

Why did Holmes think this?

TYING THE KNOT

I had been telling Holmes about a visit I had once had from an American acquaintance, when he sprung a rather odd question on me:

"Watson," he asked, "do you suppose that it is legal in New York for a man to marry his widow's sister?"

"Legal? Well, yes," I replied, "but frowned upon, I should think."

At this Holmes chuckled. "Frowned upon, indeed! Oh, Watson, you do amuse me."

Why did Holmes find my answer so funny?

A Table Tennis Trick

After the successful closure of a case, Holmes and I had been compelled to attend a celebratory dinner at the house of the wealthy client (much to Holmes' annoyance, it might be added). After dinner, it was suggested that we try out their new table tennis set. Unfortunately, however, there was only one ball to be found, and a particularly vigorous shot from a certain detective's assistant sent it flying out of the window, where it fell into a hole in a large stone garden feature. This hole was far too narrow for any of us to reach in and pick up the ball, and was too deep and dark for us to see exactly where it had come to rest. And yet, using only resources readily available to us, Holmes was able to retrieve the ball undamaged. How did he do it? I should also note that he did not damage the stone feature in any way.

THE COLOURED CUBE

"Watson," said Holmes, "I am picturing a cube with each face either completely red or completely blue."

"That sounds like a waste of your mental talents," I replied.

"You are quite right, Watson, but it's your mental talents that concern me at this precise moment."

"Well I do wish they would stop concerning you quite so much!" I responded, exasperatedly.

"The more of these puzzles we do, the less concerned I will be," he chided. "Now, listen. About this cube: I want you to tell me how many possible combinations of face arrangements it could possibly have. To clarify, if one combination can be rotated so that it matches another combination, we will consider those the same combination."

"I must say, Holmes, with all these puzzles you throw at me I sometimes think you look forward to seeing my face completely red."

"Now, now, Watson, don't look so blue. This isn't a difficult one."

How many possible combinations are there?

A Textile Teaser

"I was visiting the old bazaar with Mrs. H the other day," remarked Holmes, "and as I passed by a clothing stand I was struck with the inspiration for a riddle – and I do know how you enjoy being perplexed by such trivial things."

"How kind," I replied, tersely.

"Tell me, Watson: what is it that is bought by the yard and yet worn by the foot?"

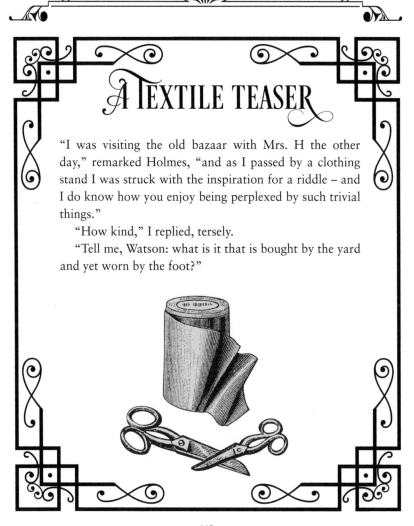

BACTERIAL GROWTH

One particularly bizarre case took Holmes and myself to a laboratory where some odd-looking cultures were being grown in Petri dishes.

"Watson," Holmes said to me, in a way that suggested he was about to demonstrate his superior intellect. "Imagine that a Petri dish contains bacteria which divide in two every minute. If I tell you that there was a single bacterium at 9 a.m. and now, two and a half hours later at 11.30 a.m., the dish is half full, then at what time will the dish be full?"

A FIFTH CODED MESSAGE

Holmes once told me that after the first twenty-four hours the probability of recovering a kidnap victim drops significantly. So when a girl named Adelia Atkins disappeared, we were under serious time pressure to find her, and could not afford to pursue all possible avenues. In terms of potential abductors, we considered her mother, Alexandra, and her father, Lucian, both of whom had been out of the city at the time of the disappearance. We also considered the nanny, Maria, who had been taking care of the girl and her brother James. And then there was the uncle, Charles, who had visited the children on the previous day.

Just before we set off from 221B to begin our investigation, we received the following note:

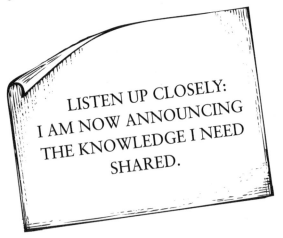

LISTEN UP CLOSELY: I AM NOW ANNOUNCING THE KNOWLEDGE I NEED SHARED.

The note then appeared to have been torn, so that whatever followed was no longer attached.

"This is useless to us in this state, isn't it, Holmes?" I asked.

Holmes took the note and examined it for a moment. "On the contrary, Watson, it tells us exactly who we need to pursue."

Who was it?

A PSYCHIC PARADOX

Given Holmes' predilection for the pseudo-supernatural, we often find ourselves encountering those who fancy themselves to have a special connection to the occult.

"I simply cannot understand why these people must carry on as though they have magical abilities," I said, after yet another such episode. "It is as plain as day to anyone with a scientific mind that prediction of the future is impossible."

"I wouldn't be so hasty, Watson," Holmes replied. "Impossible is a strong word. Why, just the other day I saw it done."

How is it possible that Holmes saw someone predict the future?

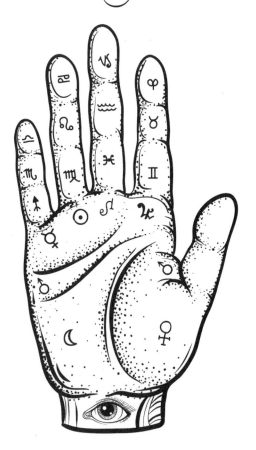

THE CROSSROADS

Holmes and I were taking a carriage through an unfamiliar stretch of English countryside when we arrived at a crossroads. Moreover, some crude vandal had pushed over the marker indicating where each road led and discarded it in a nearby ditch, so we had no clue as to in which way our destination lay.

"What a bothersome thing to do!" I exclaimed, and our driver was quite in agreement.

"Now Watson, there's no need to get heated," said Holmes. "It's just a harmless prank."

"Harmless? We'll have to wait here for hours until someone comes along who can give us directions!"

"That would be quite unnecessary."

Holmes was right, of course. So how could we determine which way we ought to go?

I rose early one Sunday morning, so I decided to make breakfast for Holmes, Mrs. Hudson and myself. The kitchen cupboards contained eggs, bacon and bread, but I thought I would ask the other two for their orders before I began cooking, so as not to cook more than was needed.

Mrs. Hudson kept things simple, requesting a piece of toast and a fried egg. Holmes, on the other hand, took the opportunity to be as cryptic as possible and, rather than saying anything, merely wrote down the following and then handed it to me:

What did Holmes want for breakfast?

A Close Shave

"Watson," Holmes said to me, "here's a little chin-scratcher for you. I interviewed a man yesterday who shaves several times a day, and yet still has all his hair."

"His aim must be terrible," I said.

But of course, that was not what was going on. What explanation did Holmes eventually reveal?

SHRINKING VOCABULARY

"Watson," Holmes once asked me, "do you not fancy yourself to be something of a linguist?"

"Well, not particularly," I replied. "You might say that I dabble, I suppose."

"In that case, I wonder what you make of this linguistic teaser: Can you think of any word that becomes smaller when you add two letters to it?"

"Of course not," I immediately rejoined. "It can't be possible. No word can get smaller when you add letters to it."

But in fact, one could. Which one?

THE MISSING PENNY

Holmes and I once had a client who refused to meet us in our offices but instead insisted on dining with us at his preferred restaurant. Despite the fact that we were there to help, he made no offer to pay for our meals, so when the bill of thirty pence came, Holmes and I had to pay our share.

Each of us handed ten pence to the waiter. A short while later, however, it transpired that we had been billed incorrectly: we in fact owed only twenty-five pence. On explaining this mistake to us, the waiter proposed that as it would be impossible to perfectly divide the five pence we were owed in return between three, he should give us each one pence back and keep two pence as a tip.

Holmes and I were rather unimpressed by this suggestion, and he later told me of his suspicion that this mistake with the bill was a cheat run by the staff at the restaurant to squeeze extra money out of gullible customers. However, at the time, we did not wish to seem miserly in front of our client, so we politely agreed.

We were all assembling our things and getting ready to leave, when our client suddenly stopped us dead.

"Just a moment!" he exclaimed, making Holmes and myself both jump.

The waiter quickly appeared at his elbow. "Is there a problem, sir?"

"There certainly is! These two gentlemen and I each paid nine pence, making a total of twenty-seven pence. You yourself received two pence. But that adds up to twenty-nine pence. And yet we gave you thirty pence! What happened to the other penny?"

The waiter, looking rather panicked at the prospect of upsetting one of his regular customers, retrieved one of the pennies of his tip and made to hand it back to us.

"That won't be necessary," said Holmes. "The explanation of what has gone on here is quite simple."

What was it?

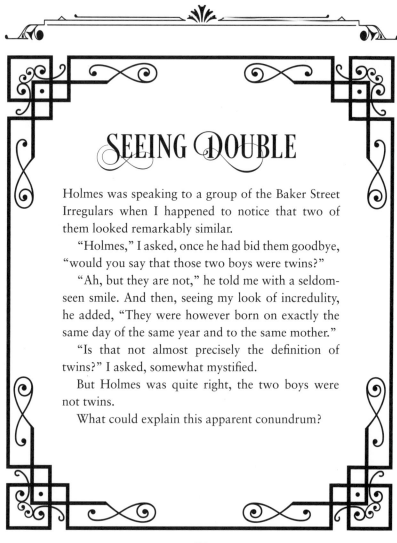

SEEING DOUBLE

Holmes was speaking to a group of the Baker Street Irregulars when I happened to notice that two of them looked remarkably similar.

"Holmes," I asked, once he had bid them goodbye, "would you say that those two boys were twins?"

"Ah, but they are not," he told me with a seldom-seen smile. And then, seeing my look of incredulity, he added, "They were however born on exactly the same day of the same year and to the same mother."

"Is that not almost precisely the definition of twins?" I asked, somewhat mystified.

But Holmes was quite right, the two boys were not twins.

What could explain this apparent conundrum?

THE MANSION MURDER

One Monday in early July, Holmes and I were summoned to a mansion about a half an hour's drive from London. The previous morning, at around eleven o'clock, a shout had been heard in the master bedroom. When the butler went upstairs to investigate he had found the master of the house, Sir Edward Wallingthorpe, lying dead on the floor, strangled by his own scarf.

Holmes and I interviewed everyone at the scene as to their whereabouts at the time of the murder, and each person had a story for us. The cook was in the kitchen, preparing lunch. The maid was in the front hallway, collecting the day's mail. Lady Wallingthorpe was in the drawing room, reading. The butler had been in the dining room, setting the table, before he went upstairs and found the body.

"That hasn't given us much to go on," I said, once we'd finished interviewing them all. "Everyone's alibi is as hard to substantiate as everyone else's. How can we tell who, if any of them, was lying?"

"With ease," said Holmes. "In fact, I'm prepared to instruct an arrest."

Who did Holmes plan to have arrested and why?

TAKING THE FALL

Holmes came in from the street with his faced flushed from the cold winter air.

"There are a large number of building works on the streets fronting Regent's Park," he informed me. "I'd steer clear of the place, if I were you. It all looks rather unsafe, and in fact I just saw a man fall backwards off a thirty-foot ladder directly onto the stone floor beneath."

"Goodness!" I exclaimed. "Was he alright?"

"Oh yes," said Holmes. "He was completely unharmed."

How was this possible?

MRS. BARKER'S CASE

Holmes and I occasionally received some rather eccentric clients. One in particular who springs to mind is Mrs. Barker, a tiny, trembling woman who arrived at our door clutching a fat, purring tabby cat to her chest. Afraid that she might topple over at any moment I hurried her to a seat, before asking how we could be of service.

"It's B-Bob and S-Sarah," she stammered. "I c-came home to find them lying on the floor, d-dead, absolutely c-covered in glass and water."

At this she dissolved into tears, and we were unable to get another word out of her on the matter. After a rather uncomfortable silence, broken only by Mrs. Barker's sobs, Holmes leaned forward and – changing the subject with uncharacteristic tact – gestured to the cat in Mrs. Barker's lap.

"What is the name of this fine specimen?"

"Mr. T-Tiddles," she replied tearfully.

Holmes reached out and solemnly shook the cat's paw, before turning to me.

"Well, Watson, it seems we have our man."

What had happened to Bob and Sarah?

Holmes and I were having a drink at a local public house one night when a last-minute change of drinks order resulted in the landlord pouring a drink from a half pint to a full pint glass.

"Watson," Holmes said, in that way that demonstrated he had just been inspired by this turn of events. "I've just thought of a rather good problem for you. Imagine that you want to measure out exactly four pints, but you only have two containers, one of which can contain precisely three pints, and the other of which can contain precisely five pints. How do you do it?" He then added, after a short pause, "I should add that you have a beer tap which you can use as much as you wish, and there is no need to worry about wasting some beer en route to your solution."

How could it be done?

AN ODD BIOGRAPHY

"I'm reading a book about a rather unusual man, Watson," said Holmes. "He turned thirty in 1740, and yet he was only twenty in 1750."

How could this be?

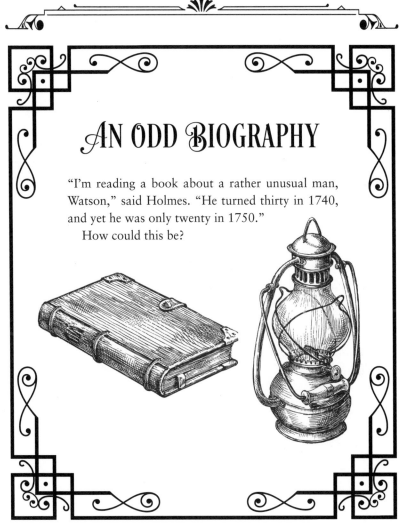

WALKING THE DOGS

Holmes and I were taking a stroll across Regent's Park when we came across a man walking three dogs.

"I'm sure I saw that chap out yesterday with three entirely different dogs," I remarked. "Perhaps people hire him to walk their dogs for them."

"What a strange concept, Watson. But in any case, that gives me an idea for an interesting puzzle," said Holmes. "Let us stipulate that this man has the care of fifteen different dogs, and, moreover, that he is charged with walking each of them every day. He doesn't like walking more than three at once, so he goes on five walks a day with three dogs in tow each time."

"I think I'm with you so far," I said, cautiously. "Where does the puzzle come in?"

"Well, if one found oneself in such a position," Holmes said, "one might naturally wonder whether it would be possible to arrange these walks so

that each individual dog is never on a walk with the same dog twice in a week."

"Naturally," I said, somewhat sarcastically. "And what might one naturally conclude on the matter?" I queried.

"Well, what do you think, Watson?" replied Holmes.

Could it be done?

THE QUATERNARY SEQUENCE

You will no doubt be pleased to hear, dear reader, that I have only one more of Holmes' sequences to report. This final time we were, I believe, in a restaurant kitchen – a very high-pressure environment in which it is most embarrassing to have a colleague who refuses to speak until you have uttered the required letter, I might add!

The sequence was as follows:

H, T, Q, F, S, S, _

What letter should come next?

DON'T PUT THE CART BEFORE THE HORSE

Holmes and I were taking a stroll down a country lane when we came across a most surprising sight. A tree on the right-hand side of the road had been torn from its roots by a recent storm, and had fallen onto a tree on the left-hand side of the road so that it hung across the road. Worse still, a horse and carriage had attempted to pass under the fallen tree but had clearly underestimated how tall the carriage was, and the carriage was now quite perfectly wedged beneath the fallen tree, unable to move either forwards or backwards.

Naturally, Holmes and I went to try and help. Even the combined strength of the two of us and the driver could shift neither the tree nor the carriage, and the driver was in any case loath to risk either damaging the carriage directly, or risk dislodging the tree from its resting place and causing it to crush the carriage.

Luckily, however, Holmes was able to make a very simple suggestion to enable the driver to get his carriage out from under the tree.

What was it?

Bottled Up

After a few drinks at a local hostelry one night, Holmes and I found ourselves with an empty wine bottle. Holmes duly dropped a small coin into the bottle, and then reinserted the cork.

"Say, Watson," he said. "I bet you the next round that I can remove the coin from this bottle without pulling out the cork or breaking the bottle."

Now, although I could see no way of doing it, I was no fool and refused Holmes the bet, knowing full well that he would somehow manage this trick. And indeed I was right.

How did he do it?

A SIXTH CODED MESSAGE

Our sixth coded message was delivered to us at a large mansion, where we were looking into an alleged haunting. The mansion was a short drive from the nearest village, and we believe that it was someone in the village who decided to help us in our investigation. Shortly after finding the shifty-

looking note we went outside to find fresh wheel markings on the driveway of the mansion.

Regardless of the identity of the writer, which we never did definitively discover, the contents of the note did eventually prove critical to locating the clever contraption that was responsible for the ghostly goings-on we had been summoned to investigate.

The note read as follows:

MPPL JO UIF
ESBXJOH SPPN

Can you decode the note?
Where did we find the contraption?

AN ENTERTAINING ENIGMA

During a particularly slow afternoon in our chambers, Holmes and I had rejoined for a hot beverage when he chose to spring another of his unexpected riddles on me.

"Here's a little puzzle to keep your brain sharp on this dullest of days, Watson," he said, with something of a twinkle in his eye. "The riddle is this: It enters dry, and yet comes out wet. The longer it's in, the stronger it gets. What is it?"

CROSSING THE THAMES

"I witnessed an entertaining sight, today, Watson," Holmes informed me. "Two boys – friends, I believe – both wished to cross the Thames. They had only a single one-person boat between them. Yet they both managed to cross in the boat, without either of them having to swim, and without them using any sort of trick to get the boat across without any occupants."

How was this possible?

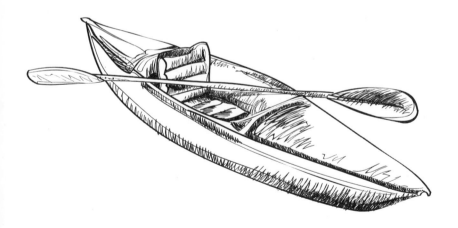

CRUMBLED UP

Holmes and I came home to find that, seized by a rare fit of enthusiasm for baking, Mrs. Hudson had decided to attempt to make some plum crumble. As we arrived, however, she was in a state of despair.

"Whatever has happened, Mrs. Hudson?" I asked her. "Is there anything we can do to help?"

"Not unless you can turn back time," she replied. "I've put all the plums in but I wasn't counting how many, and now it turns out that the amount of sugar you need to add is proportional to the number of plums. It's ruined! And they were such nice plums too."

"I'm sure it's not too important," I assured her. "A rough estimate will do."

"No need for that," said Holmes. "Mrs. Hudson, I believe we can determine exactly how many plums you put in the crumble."

What strategy did he have in mind?

A LONG YEAR

"And how old are you?" I asked Mrs. Hudson's youngest great nephew.

"I'll be turning seven next year!" he told me, flushed with pride and keen, as children so often are, to seem older than they really are.

"And to think," said his older sister, "that he was only four years old the day before yesterday."

Is it possible that both of their statements are true?

THE ONE RULE

I was sitting down to dinner with Holmes one night when he suddenly removed the salt from the table.

"Watson, I'm imposing a rule on you, until such time as you determine what that rule is."

I sighed, but did not bother protesting.

"You are allowed pepper, but not salt. You are allowed beef but no lamb. Carrots, yes, cabbage and broccoli if you so desire, but no potato, in any form. Oh, and you must eat with a spoon."

What was the rule?

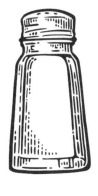

THE THREE CHILDREN

Holmes once had a visit from an old acquaintance whom I had never met before. I found them chatting freely in a way he seldom did with me as I came in to offer them some tea.

"And how are your children?" Holmes was asking. "You have three, if I remember rightly, although I must admit I don't quite recall their ages."

"You always enjoyed deduction, didn't you, old chap?" his acquaintance replied. "What if I told you that the product of their ages was 40?"

"That's not quite enough information for me to deduce their ages," said Holmes.

"Alright, well I shall add that the sum of their ages is the number of years we've known each other."

Holmes considered this. "I'll still need a tad more."

"Finally, the youngest was our first summer baby, born in July."

"Ah, I see."

Holmes suddenly turned to me. "Why don't you tell this gentleman the ages of his children, then, Watson?"

I balked. "But I don't know how long you've known each other!"

"That doesn't matter, Watson! You now have enough information to deduce it."

And indeed I did. How old are the three children?

KEEPING CLEAN

Holmes and I were consulting with a couple of the Baker Street Irregulars when a sudden gust of wind picked up some dirt from the ground and blew it towards their faces, covering one boy's face in dirt and yet somehow leaving the other's completely clean. But strangely enough, it was the boy with the clean face who ran to a nearby water barrel to wash his face, while the other remained where he was.

I turned to Holmes with a quizzically raised eyebrow but, as usual, Holmes was unsurprised.

What explanation did Holmes provide?

THE FAMILY NAME

"I ran into an old acquaintance today, Watson," Holmes informed me, as we sat at the dinner table.

"That's always a pleasant surprise," I replied. "Had it been a long time since you had last seen one another?"

"Quite," Holmes replied. "It was in fact closing in on fifteen years."

"Goodness, why that's almost half a lifetime," I exclaimed.

"A whole lifetime, for some," said Holmes, rather sadly. "In any case, as it turns out my friend had married ten years ago, to someone I have never met, and today I was introduced to their eight-year-old daughter."

"How sweet," I said. "What was her name?"

"I asked the girl the same thing and, as is typical of children, she didn't give me a plain answer. Instead she told me it was the same as her mother's, and of course that was enough."

"How was that enough to establish her name, if you have never met her mother?"

"My dear Watson," Holmes exclaimed, "I believe you've made another one of your fallacious inferences."

What was my mistake?

THE FOURTH REBUS

One morning, Holmes failed to make his usual curmudgeonly appearance at the breakfast table. He had worked late into the night, so I did not want to risk awakening his acerbic wrath by knocking on his bedroom door and enquiring as to whether anything was the matter. But as morning became afternoon, however, I began to worry, so I tentatively tapped on the frame of his door. He said nothing that I heard, but a folded piece of paper soon pushed itself out from under his door.

It read:

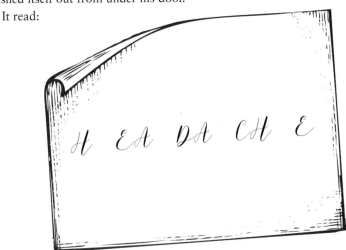

What was he communicating?

AN UNCRACKABLE SEQUENCE

Sitting down to wait for Holmes in his office one day, my eye strayed across a piece of paper with one of his infernal sequences on it. This one was made up of numbers, which read as follows: 16 06 68 88. Feeling certain that he had left it there on purpose to vex me, I set about trying to work out what could possibly link the numbers, but in truth I sat there for a good half an hour and yet still the answer eluded me.

Finally, Holmes came in, and saw me struggling.

"Go on then, Holmes," I said to him. "Put me out of my misery. What's the connection here?"

Holmes laughed. "Why, Watson, it's the very simplest of sequences."

And once he told me, I saw that he was right. What connected the numbers?

A PRIESTLY POSER

Holmes and I once tackled a case that involved the disappearance of a priest, and at one point our investigations brought us to a remote hilltop chapel.

"Watson," Holmes said, as we began our ascent up the broad stone steps, "consider this. A priest sets off at nine a.m. up a path to a hilltop chapel, and arrives at nine p.m. The following day, he sets off at nine a.m., and reaches the bottom at nine p.m. Is there any moment on the second day at which he is at exactly the same step on the path at exactly the same time as he was on the previous day?"

I frowned. "Surely that depends on his speed, and whether he took breaks at any point on either day," I answered. "How can you possibly know the answer without more information?"

"Know?" he replied. "I can do one better. I can prove it."

What was Holmes' proof?

THE LONG THROW

Holmes found an old tennis ball of mine lying about our chambers, which I presume prompted him to put the following challenge to me: "Watson, how would you throw this ball as hard as you can so that, without bouncing it off anything or it being caught and returned by anyone, it is certain to always come straight back to you?"

How was I to do it?

A SEVENTH CODED MESSAGE

The seventh coded message we received concerned a client of ours named Mr. Alexander. Mr. Alexander ran a restaurant in a well-to-do part of the city, but he came to us because he had noticed that his figures weren't adding up: someone was stealing money as it made its way from the tables to the cash repository.

In his employment were seven people: Frank Pale, the chef; Martin Heal, the head waiter; Janet Bars, a waitress; Richard, Charlie and Mark Sharp, the bussers; and David Pound, the sommelier. Any one of them could be the thief.

It was midway through our investigation that we received the following anonymous tip-off:

HE SARP BRS PAL
ALEXNDER'S POUND.
-THOMAS

We asked Mr. Alexander if he knew anyone called Thomas, and he told us he did not. But curiously it was this very fact that led Holmes to crack the code.

Who was responsible for the missing money?

RUNNING IN CIRCLES

"Watson," Holmes said to me one day as we were walking down Baker Street, "have you ever noticed that removable manhole covers are almost always circular in shape?"

"I must say I'd never really thought about it," I replied, "but now you point it out I can see that it's true."

"I suppose," said Holmes somewhat pensively, "that if you reflect on the matter for a moment it turns out to be not in the least surprising."

What reason did Holmes see for removable manhole covers needing to be round rather than square or rectangular?

The Long Corridor

"How about a little breakfast brainteaser?" Holmes asked me the other morning, peering out from behind his newspaper.

I knew better than to bother protesting, so I waited for him to continue.

"There is a corridor lined with one hundred doors. One hundred people are waiting at one end. The first person goes through the corridor and opens every door. The second goes through and shuts every second door. The third changes every third door – shutting it if it's open, and opening if it's shut. The fourth changes every fourth door, the fifth every fifth, and so on, right up until the one hundredth person, who only changes the very last door. Given all of this activity, can you say which doors will be open at the end of this process?"

Sighing, I reached for my pen and began marking out the doors on my own newspaper, so as to work my way through them one by one.

"No, no, Watson," Holmes said, waving his hand dismissively at me. "There's no need for copious note-taking. The answer is really very simple when you consider the question properly."

Can you see what Holmes meant?

A Miss Juliet Williams had sought out Holmes' services to help retrieve some valuable jewels which had apparently vanished from her locked cabinet. A little investigation had led us to suspect her brother-in-law, and we were beginning to close in on him when she received the following message in the post from her brother-in-law:

What did it say?

A CITRUS CONUNDRUM

The mother of a certain client of ours was suffering from some rather inexplicable symptoms, which Holmes hypothesized to be the result of an unknown, exotic poison. It was as a result of this that we found ourselves walking through Kew Gardens, examining some of the more unusual plants and reading of their properties. Holmes had reason to suspect an uncle who had recently returned from India, so we were taking particular note of any plants he might have obtained on his travels.

After a long period of silent note-taking, Holmes suddenly turned to me with a strange twinkle in his eye.

"Watson, I'm thinking of a plant."

"I'm not surprised," I replied. "Do you think you've identified the murder weapon?"

"No, no," he smiled. "This is an unrelated matter."

"Okay, well what plant is it then?" I asked.

"I shall give you a clue: it's an arboreal citrus plant."

I could tell by his face that he had some grand dénouement in store for me, but I was unable to work out what he was getting at.

"I give up Holmes, what is it?"

Can you guess the plant that Holmes was thinking of?

DEARLY BELOVED

"I met a man the other day who has married over a hundred women," Holmes announced to me one day.

"Well that's clearly entirely inappropriate!" I replied. "After a certain number of divorces, surely one must realize that one is not the marrying kind."

"Oh, but on the contrary, my dear Watson, the man has never divorced, and all the women are quite happy."

What perfectly logical explanation was Holmes able to offer for this? The man was not, I might add, a polygamist.

THE TREACHEROUS TRAP

Holmes and I received a message from Inspector Lestrade concerning a recent murder that had taken place in West London. George Anderson had been found dead in his flat in Hammersmith, and the police had reason to believe the murderer was extremely dangerous, so they told us they were sending an armed escort to take us to the crime scene.

When the doorbell eventually rang, we were greeted by a heavily built young man with a large nose and thick eyebrows. We got into a carriage with him and were driven out west to Hammersmith. I have to say I was a little nervous about the whole affair, but I had insisted on accompanying Holmes, so I was sure not to let on.

When we arrived, our police escort produced a key and unlocked the front door. Behind it was a small hallway with several doors opening off it, and a narrow flight of stairs at the end.

"This way," he said, gesturing to the distant staircase. "The body's on the upstairs floor, not down here."

At these words Holmes froze, and turned to me. "Watson," he said very quietly, "I believe this is a trap. Let us try to retreat without him noticing."

We managed to escape, and it did transpire that the man who had shown us to the house had not been sent by the police. But how did Holmes know?

SOLUTIONS

Tom was the boy with bushy hair, and had worked on The Case of the Vanishing Glass. Mickey was the boy with the scar under his eye, and had worked on The Crimson Consideration, while Joe was the boy with the mole on his chin, and had worked on The Mark of Three.

It's the only number which contains all ten digits in alphabetical order.

The train to Leicester leaves two minutes earlier than the train to Dover. There are therefore only two minutes out of every twenty during which the Dover train is the next to leave, or in other words, the Dover train is only the next to leave ten per cent of the time.

The Earl had looked up to see the woman framed brightly in sunlight through the doorway, in front of the whitewashed wall. As he blinked, she happened to walk away, leaving him with the bright inverse afterglow that appears whenever you have looked at a brightly lit object. Against the whitewashed wall, he saw the glowing complementary hue of her dress, turning the vivid green into a brilliant, shining red.

Lunch and dinner.

SOLUTIONS

Four By Four

There are multiple possibilities for some numbers but there is at least one way of making every number from 1 to 20:

$1 = \frac{4}{4} \times \frac{4}{4}$

$2 = \frac{4}{4} + \frac{4}{4}$

$3 = \frac{4 + 4 + 4}{4}$

$4 = 4 + 4 (4 - 4)$

$5 = \frac{(4 \times 4) + 4}{4}$

$6 = \frac{4!}{4} \times \frac{4}{4}$

$7 = (4 + 4) - \frac{4}{4}$

$8 = 4(\frac{4 + 4}{4})$

$9 = \frac{4}{4} + 4 + 4$

$10 = (\frac{4}{\sqrt{4}}) + (4 \times \sqrt{4})$

$11 = (\frac{(4! \times \sqrt{4}) - 4}{4})$

$12 = 4(4 - \frac{4}{4})$

$13 = (\frac{(4! \times \sqrt{4}) + 4}{4})$

$14 = 4 \times (\sqrt{4} + \sqrt{4}) - \sqrt{4}$

$15 = (4 \times 4) - \frac{4}{4}$

$16 = (4 \times 4) + 4 - 4$

$17 = (4 \times 4) + \frac{4}{4}$

$18 = (4 \times 4) + 4 - \sqrt{4}$

$19 = 4! - (4 + \frac{4}{4})$

$20 = 4 \times (4 + \frac{4}{4})$

A Mysterious Place

A map.

The Present-Packing Poser

Yes – I could pack the parcels in the following way:
Crate one: 15 pound parcel and 10 pound parcel.
Crate two: 13 pound parcel, 11 pound parcel, and 1 pound parcel.
Crate three: 9 pound parcel, 8 pound parcel, 4 pound parcel and two 2 pound parcels.

Great Nieces and Great Nephews

This rule would not change the biological probability of having a girl from being 50 per cent, so would not affect the gender ratio. It would simply affect how many children a particular couple might have.

SOLUTIONS

Holmes removed the lid of the barrel and then tipped the barrel so the beer was level with the lowest part of the top of the barrel. As the bottom of the barrel was not at all visible when he did this, they could be sure that the landlord was right: the barrel was more than half full. Had some of the bottom of the barrel been visible, this would have vindicated the customer instead.

They both have four children.

He simply read only during daylight hours.

A yardstick.

Somewhat aptly, TYPEWRITER is one of the longest words you can type. It is not alone among ten-letter words, however, since PERPETUITY, PREREQUIRE, PROPRIETOR and REPERTOIRE are also possible.

Yes, it was possible. To create every number from 1 to 31, you need the following twelve digits: 0, 1, 1, 2, 2, 3, 4, 5, 6, 7, 8, 9, which as you will see fit perfectly onto the twelve faces of two cubes. There must be a 1 and a 2 on each cube, and the 0 and the 3 must be on different cubes.

6,210,001,000

Mrs. Hudson's sister is 60. (Her children are 40, 37, 34, and 31.)

SOLUTIONS

The Secret Message 36

I was to send the box to Holmes with my padlock on it. When he received it, he could then attach a padlock of his own to the box and send it back. When I then received it, I could then unlock my original lock and send it back to him with only his own padlock on it.

The Bamboozling Bacon 37

The quickest possible time (ignoring time taken to switch/flip rashers) is three minutes. This can be achieved by frying slices 1 and 2 on one side for one minute, then removing 1, flipping 2 and frying 3 for one minute (so 2 is now done on both sides), and then frying the other side of 1 and 3 for one minute.

The Second Deduction 38

Agatha and Beatrice are Mrs. Hudson's nieces, and Jane and Margaret are Agatha's daughters (and therefore Mrs. Hudson's great nieces).

The Primary Sequence 41

The next letter is U. The sequence is first letters of planets in the solar system, starting with the closest to the sun and moving outwards.

A Card Conundrum 42

The probability is 1/33. This is obtained from dividing the probability that both are twos (4/52 x 3/51 = 12/(51x52)) by the probability that one is a two (396/(51x52)).

Red and Green Apples 44

The best strategy is to put a single red apple into one of the sacks and the rest of the apples in the other sack. That way, one sack gives a 100% chance of picking a red apple and the other gives a 48.7% chance; overall, this is a 74.3% chance of getting a red apple.

SOLUTIONS

Even More Apples 45

One of the apples you give away can be given while still in the sack.

The Long Walk 46

He walked to Paris, Texas, not Paris, France.

Clipped Wings 48

A caterpillar has no wings, but will one day be able to fly when it becomes a moth or butterfly.

The Impatient Pocket Watch 50

It was twenty-four minutes past one. When it is actually 1pm, Watson's watch shows 2:40pm. And when it is actually 2pm, Watson's watch shows 3:45pm. Currently the watch shows 3:06pm, which means the real time is sometime between 1pm and 2pm. To calculate the number of minutes past the hour, note that they are 26 minutes into the 65 minute 'hour' shown by the watch. Because the watch runs 5 minutes fast per hour, this means that every 12 minutes of real time the watch advances 13 minutes. So these 26 left-over minutes on the watch correspond to 2x13 minutes of watch time, or 2x12 minutes of real-time. Therefore the time is 1:24pm.

Celebrity Conundrum 52

Surnames.

The Third Deduction 54

In The Adventure of the Broken Table, Sarah Doyle was robbed by Peter Watkins. In The Adventure of the Frozen Lake, Mark Robinson was murdered by Charlotte Green. In The Adventure of the Moving Statue, John Bell was defrauded by Juliet Lane.

SOLUTIONS

Back ache.

Wherever you find something is always the last place you look because once you've found it, you simply stop looking!

This is possible in seventeen minutes. First, Holmes and Lestrade cross over, which takes two minutes. Then Lestrade goes back with the torch, taking another two minutes. Next, Mrs. Hudson and I cross, which takes ten minutes. Then Holmes goes back with the torch, taking another minute, and finally, Holmes and Lestrade cross over for the final time, taking another two minutes. This brings the total time to seventeen minutes.

The longest commonly used words are ALASKA, FLASKS, SALADS and SALSAS. Longer than those are ALFALFAS, plants in the pea family, and HAGGADAH, a Jewish text.

I simply need to pour the contents of the second glass into the fifth glass and then return the second glass to its original position.

There were fourteen biscuits on the children's plate.

COME TO FIFTEEN JUNIPER STREET. The spaces between the words have been changed, and unnecessary line breaks added.

SOLUTIONS

Another Card Conundrum

Yes, it does make a difference. In the first case, as you may recall, the probability is 1/33, whereas in the second case, when we know it's a two of hearts specifically, the probability is 1/17, obtained from dividing the probability that both are twos and one is the two of hearts (6/(51x52)) by the probability that one is the two of hearts ((51+51)/(51x52)). In other words, in the second case, the probability of drawing two twos is almost twice as high. Knowing that one of the cards is a two of hearts, rather than just any two, narrows down the number of possible combinations in which both cards are a two, since combinations such as the two of diamonds and the two of spades are ruled out. What's more, it narrows down the number of possible combinations in which it is not the case that both cards are twos, since combinations such as the two of diamonds and the three of diamonds are then ruled out. So, knowing that you have a two of hearts gives you a much better chance of getting two twos than just knowing you have a two.

The Mixed-Up Label

Mrs. Hudson should take a spoonful from the jar labelled 'MIXED'. If she tastes sugar, she will know that this was the jar of pure sugar, meaning the jar labelled 'SALT' must be the mixed jar and the jar labelled 'SUGAR' must be the salt jar. If she tastes salt, she would likewise know that this was the jar of pure salt, meaning the jar labelled 'SALT' must be the sugar jar and the jar labelled 'SUGAR' must be the mixed jar.

The Two Dentists

Given that there are only two dentists in the town, we can assume that they are each other's dentists. In this case, the dentist with the better teeth can be inferred to be the worse dentist, since he will be treated by the other dentist.

SOLUTIONS

The words that Holmes found are cede, cited, deceit, deceive, detect, device, dice, die, diet, dive, edict, edit, evicted, iced, teed, tide, tied, vetted and vied, plus the nine-letter word 'detective'.

The next letter is S. The sequence consists of the first letters of days of the week, starting from Tuesday.

The book was stolen by Nicholas Richardson, since it can be deduced he was the third person to visit the archives. As the old man says, the book was still there for the entirety of the second person's visit.

Holmes had added sugar to his tea before he saw the fly. As soon as he tasted the 'new' cup, he could tell it was the same one, because it already had sugar in it.

The subscription for *The Needlepoint Nut* works out to be much cheaper than that of *The Fowl Fanatic*, even after one year but certainly after four.

There was one rose, one tulip and one geranium.

All of these words have their letters in alphabetical order.

SOLUTIONS

The trick is to realize that the coins can be put on top of each other, and not just flat on the table. Once you realize this, you can place three coins flat on the table, each one touching the other two in a triangular formation, and then put the fourth on top of them.

The Clock Tower is 105 yards tall.

The man was in the uniform of a hansom cab driver and so was clearly a driver, but at that time he wasn't actually driving – he was simply walking.

Including the two I spoke to, there were a total of four sisters and three brothers.

He's under arrest. (HEs under a rest)

Ask the guard whether the other guard would say that this is the right door. If it is the right door, then either guard will answer "no". If it is the wrong door, then either guard will answer "yes".

Magnets. The box appeared to get much heavier when on a metal table, which could be caused by the contents of the box being magnetically attracted to the table.

SOLUTIONS

I could eat all three cakes from the largest tin, and then place the smallest tin inside the now empty largest one. This way, each tin would still contain three cakes.

10 ounces. One per cent of 20 is 0.2, so the clothes on their own must weigh 0.2 ounces. If 0.2 ounces make up two per cent of the overall weight, the overall weight must be 10 ounces.

I said to Holmes, "You will not give me a plain or a raisin biscuit." Holmes could not then give me nothing, as that would make my statement true, nor could he give a plain or raisin biscuit, as that would make my statement false: his only remaining option was to give me the chocolate chip biscuit I desired.

Four men.

In the basement of 9 Camden Road. The message has its 'A's swapped with its 'E's and its 'I's swapped with its 'O's. The decoded message thus reads: THE ARTWORK YOU SEEK IS IN THE BASEMENT OF NINE CAMDEN ROAD.

Red was shipping diamonds from the East storehouse on Monday. Yellow was shipping rubies from the South storehouse on Tuesday. Blue was shipping emeralds from the North storehouse on Wednesday. Green was shipping sapphires from the West storehouse on Thursday.

SOLUTIONS

An Odd Order

They were standing back to back.

Sleeping It Off

If the husband died on the spot, he wouldn't have been able to report his dream to anyone.

The Case of the Secret Sailors

The password was WELCOME. The clocks on the wall represented flag semaphore characters spelling out this word.

Getting the Chop

Meat. I am still unclear whether this was a joke on Holmes' part or a genuine misunderstanding: both seem equally unlikely.

Irregular Twins

The day was the 29th of February. If the twins were born on either side of midnight of the 28th of February, on a non-leap year, then on a leap year their birthdays would be two days apart.

A Puddle Puzzle

A towel.

The Strange Shipwreck

As they are survivors, they won't be buried at all. Or at least not any time soon, hopefully.

The Tertiary Sequence

The next letter is R. The sequence consists of the last letters of months of the year.

SOLUTIONS

A Palindromic Puzzle 119

The next palindromic number would be 25,052, which is 110 more than 24,942.

Racing Results. 120

If a dog in second place is overtaken, the dog overtaking is now in second place, not first place.

If a dog is in last place then a dog overtaking it must have lapped the others, and it could be in any position other than last.

Carnival Cakes. 121

The actual weight of the cake was 72 ounces, meaning that my guess was the closest, and Holmes admitted I had beaten him for perhaps the only time in my life.

Holmes, Scrambled. 122

The twelve-letter word (re-using letters) is COCKLESHELLS. A few eleven-letter ones are CHROMOSOMES, HORSESHOERS, REMORSELESS, SCHOOLROOMS and SORCERESSES. The nine-letter word is HORSESHOE.

Matching Socks 125

Taking seven socks would ensure at least three matching pairs. Even if Watson picked out seven socks of the same colour then he would have three matching pairs (and one extra), so he would fulfil the requirements.

Common Property Two. 126

All of these words can be either a noun or a verb, and are pronounced differently in each case.

SOLUTIONS

An Illuminating Problem 128

I needed to turn the first switch on for a few minutes and then turn it off again. I was then to turn the second switch on and leave the third off. After that, I was to go down into the cellar. If the light was on, I would know it was the second switch that lit the cellar. If the light was off, I should then feel the bulb. If it was warm then I would know that it had recently been on, and was therefore controlled by the first switch. If not, it must be controlled by the third switch.

A Strangely Shaped Riddle 130
A key.

Truth-tellers and Liars 131

Yes, he should. There are two scenarios: either the woman is a Truth-teller or she is a Liar. If she is a Truth-teller, then the right-hand side of the conditional – 'I am a Truth-teller' – is true, so she will go to dinner. Alternatively, if the woman is a Liar, then the right-hand side of the conditional – 'I am a Truth-teller' – is false and she says she will not go to dinner, but we know she is lying so in fact she will go to dinner.
Either way, it is true that she will go to dinner with him.

The Poisoned Party 132

The poison was in the ice in the punch. When the Colonel drank his glass of punch the ice hadn't yet melted, but later in the party it did, which was when the poison was released into the punch and those who drank it were poisoned.

A Third Coded Message 135

It was to inform us that Mark knew who did it. The question mark was intended to read as the words 'Question Mark', giving: QUESTION MARK: HE KNOWS WHO DID IT.

SOLUTIONS

The two opposite sides of a die always add up to seven. So Holmes merely needed to add seven to the total he could see in front of him to get my overall total.

It was driven over in winter, when the lake was frozen over.

ROGERS BROTHER STRANGLED PROFESSOR BURNS. All but the first and last letter of each word have been put in reverse order.

A pillow.

My best bet is to choose the lions. If they haven't been fed for five weeks they are almost certainly dead, and if not then they must be very weak!

A complete set of dominoes will join together to form a complete ring. By secretly removing a piece before the children started joining them, Holmes was able to guarantee that the numbers at either end of the line were the same as those on the removed piece.

A book's pages are numbered starting from the right-hand side, meaning that page 48 would be on the back of page 47 and nothing could be between them.

SOLUTIONS

The Party Problem 148

Holmes' thought was that the cake could be sliced into four using two cuts from top to bottom, in the usual way, and then cut a third time across the middle, halving each of the initial four slices.

Bridge, Interrupted 151

The dealer should deal from the bottom of the pack and go around anticlockwise, starting with himself.

Atop the Shipping Container 152

As the taller of the two of us, Holmes has the longer arms, so was able to reach higher than I could have done.

Newspaper Pages 154

Page 28 is on the same sheet as pages 9, 10 and 27.

Truth-tellers and Liars Two 155

He should claim to be a poor Liar. This means he cannot be a poor Liar, or he would be telling the truth. He also cannot be a Truth-teller, since he would then be telling the truth and she does not want him to be a Truth-teller. So, of the available options, he must be a rich Liar.

A Fair Race 156

The taller boy would still win. The first race demonstrated that the taller boy could run 50 yards in the time it took the shorter boy to run 45 yards. So if the taller boy started five yards behind, they would draw level five yards from the end of the race, the taller boy having run 50 yards and the shorter 45 yards. As the taller boy is faster, he would run the final five yards more quickly, and win the race.

SOLUTIONS

Apples are normally 2 pence each, bananas 4 pence and oranges 8 pence, so the total cost for one of each would be 14 pence.

The first bullet would be shot immediately, not after ten seconds. So in a minute, at a rate of ten seconds per shot, he should manage seven shots.

60 times. Note that it's easy to count 55, 155, 255 as one digit when there are two in each.

If the witness had only seen the attacker from behind, he would not have been able to see the paint on the front of his dungarees. So the witness must have either lied in his testimony or already known in some other way that the attacker had paint on the front of his dungarees.

For a man to have a widow, he must be dead. Therefore he is quite incapable of marriage.

Holmes filled the crack with water. This caused the air-filled ball to rise to the top, where we could easily pick it up.

There are ten possible combinations: a) zero blue faces, b) zero red faces, c) one blue face, d) one red face, e) two blue faces that are adjacent, f) two blue faces that are opposite each other, g) two red faces that are adjacent, h) two red faces that are opposite each other, i) three red faces that all share one vertex, and j) three red faces, two of which are opposite each other.

SOLUTIONS

A Textile Teaser...169

A carpet.

Bacterial Growth..171

If the Petri dish is half full at 11.30 a.m., then it will be completely full when all the bacteria divide in two a minute later, at 11.31 a.m.

A Fifth Coded Message.......................................172

Lucian Atkins. The name was spelled out by the first letter of every word in the message.

A Psychic Paradox...174

It is certainly possible to predict the future – it's getting it right that's the difficult part!

The Crossroads..176

We just needed to retrieve the marker and turn it so the place we'd just come from was correctly indicated. The other destinations would then also be correctly indicated.

The Third Rebus...177

Scrambled eggs.

A Close Shave...178

The man was a barber.

Shrinking Vocabulary..179

The word 'small' becomes 'smaller' when you add 'er' to the end.

SOLUTIONS

The initial figure of thirty pence is irrelevant to the transaction. In actual fact, the two pence given to the waiter is not something extra on top of the twenty-seven pence paid, but is rather the difference between the twenty-seven pence paid and the corrected twenty-five pence bill.

The two boys were not twins but rather triplets.

Holmes planned to arrest the maid. She claimed to be collecting the mail, but the murder happened on a Sunday, so there would not have been any mail to collect.

He had been on the bottom rung of the ladder when he fell.

Bob and Sarah were goldfish, and Mr. Tiddles had pushed their bowl onto the floor.

Start by filling the five-pint container, and then pouring it into the three-pint container, thus leaving two pints in the five-pint container. Next, empty the three-pint container and pour the two pints from the five-pint container into it. Then completely fill the five-pint container again, and pour this quantity into the three-pint container until it is full. You will be left with exactly four pints in the five-pint container.

The man was born in 1770 BC.

SOLUTIONS

Walking the Dogs 192

It can certainly be done. Identifying the fifteen dogs as A to O, here is one such arrangement:

Monday	Tuesday	Wednesday	Thursday	Friday	Saturday	Sunday
A-F-K	A-B-E	B-C-F	E-F-I	C-E-K	E-G-M	K-M-D
B-G-L	C-D-G	D-E-H	G-H-K	D-F-L	F-H-N	L-N-E
C-H-M	H-I-L	I-J-M	L-M-A	G-I-O	I-K-B	O-B-H
D-I-N	J-K-N	K-L-O	N-O-C	H-J-A	J-L-C	A-C-I
E-J-O	M-O-F	N-A-G	B-D-J	M-N-B	O-A-D	F-G-J

The Quaternary Sequence 195

The next letter is E. The sequence consists of the first letters of fractions with increasing denominators: half (1/2), third (1/3), quarter (1/4), fifth (1/5), and so on.

Don't Put the Cart Before the Horse 196

Holmes suggested that the man release the air from the wheels of his carriage in order to reduce its height and allow it to be freed from the tree.

Bottled Up 198

Holmes pushed the cork into the bottle. He was then able to tip out the coin.

A Sixth Coded Message 200

In the drawing room. The message was encoded by shifting every letter by one letter alphabetically. The decoded message read: LOOK IN THE DRAWING ROOM.

SOLUTIONS

Tea.

The boys began on opposite sides of the Thames.

Holmes suggested counting the stones of the plums, which, of course, had not been added to the crumble.

Yes, if the statements were made on the 1st January, and the boy's birthday was the previous day. That way, he could have been four on the 30th December, turned five on the 31st December, be due to turn six on the 31st December of the current year, and due to turn seven on the 31st December of the next year.

I was only allowed items containing the same letter repeated consecutively.

The children are 1, 5, and 8. Given that Holmes couldn't deduce their ages despite knowing the sum of their ages, I could have worked out that the sum of their ages was 14. This is because from all the possible combinations that would yield the product of 40, only two have the same sum: 1, 5, 8, and 2, 2, 10. The final clue was necessary to choose between these two options. If two of the children were 2, then they would have to be twins. The final clue rules out this possibility.

SOLUTIONS

The boy with the clean face saw the boy with the dirty face and assumed his own face was dirty too, whereas the boy with the dirty face saw the boy with the clean face and made the opposite assumption.

The friend Holmes ran into was the girl's mother.

He had a splitting headache.

I was looking at the piece of paper upside down. It in fact read: 88 89 90 91.

Imagine there are two priests both setting off at nine a.m.: one from the top of the path and one from the bottom. For them to both reach the other end of the path at nine p.m., they must cross each other at some point. The necessity of this crossing proves that the priest from Holmes' question must have at some point been in the same place at the same time on the second day as he was on the first.

I needed to throw the ball straight up vertically into the air.

SOLUTIONS

A Seventh Coded Message 220

The Sharp Brothers. The word THOMAS indicates the letters missing from the words in the main message, and their position. So a T is the first letter of the first word, and H the second letter of the second word, and so on. The decoded message reads: THE SHARP BROS PALM ALEXANDER'S POUNDS.

Running in Circles 223

A round manhole cover cannot fall into the hole, whereas a square or a rectangular one could. It may also be noted that a circular manhole cover can be easily rolled, which could facilitate moving it.

The Long Corridor 224

The open doors would be doors 1, 4, 9, 16, 25, 36, 49, 64, 81 and 100, or in other words, the square-numbered doors. This is because these are the only numbers with an odd number of factors, so they are changed by an odd number of people and end up being left open.

The Fifth Rebus 226

Forgive and forget.

A Citrus Conundrum 228

"Why, it is a lemon tree, my dear Watson." (Elementary, my dear Watson)

Dearly Beloved 231

The man was a priest.

The Treacherous Trap 232

We were supposed to be taken to the crime scene, which was the flat where George Anderson was murdered. The place to which we were taken was clearly a multi-floor residence, and therefore could not have been the flat.